What readers are saying
Healing Your Wounded Soul

No one, Christian or not, can go through life without experiencing some form of brokenness. Father Joshua's book is uniquely helpful in that it assists the person recovering from trauma along the path of recovery while keeping an Orthodox perspective, focused as it is on the wholeness of the human being as revealed in Christ. Even people who are not actively struggling with recovering from trauma should read this book, both to understand the path being trodden by their brothers and sisters and to turn over some of the stones in the dark corners of their own souls, so that the light of Christ might truly enlighten all.

—Athanasios

Father Joshua Makoul has written a beautiful invitation and guide to healing the wounded soul—which is, in fact, all of us. His insights from psychology and the healing wisdom of the Orthodox Church are intertwined in such a way that there is no tension between them at all, as well there shouldn't be. His words radiate compassion, nonjudgment, and kindness as he lays out simple-to-apply ways to begin discerning one's woundedness, along with concrete ways to begin moving toward healing.

—Mary

Father Joshua Makoul's book *Healing Your Wounded Soul* was incredibly instrumental in my personal journey of healing from past trauma. It was a powerful catalyst that propelled me to look inward and face the pain and brokenness I had been carrying subconsciously for many years. It led me on a long journey in my efforts to process and master painful memories and begin a long overdue healing process. By the grace of God I am able to break away from reenacting old patterns and break the cycle of generational dysfunction, while extending forgiveness to myself and others and finding a true freedom in Jesus Christ.

—Anelia

HEALING WORK

Giving Humanity a Second Chance

JOSHUA MAKOUL

ANCIENT FAITH PUBLISHING

CHESTERTON, INDIANA

Healing Work: Giving Humanity a Second Chance
Copyright © 2022 Joshua Makoul

Published by:
  Ancient Faith Publishing
  A Division of Ancient Faith Ministries
  P.O. Box 748
  Chesterton, IN 46304

ISBN: 978-1-955890-21-2

Library of Congress Control Number: 2022943161

To the community of Saint George Cathedral in Pittsburgh
whose warmth and love heal
and which is a place that has no memory
for they always incline toward hope and that which is right

Contents

Introduction

WE LIVE IN A CULTURE of extremes, so we tend to acknowledge and express only two, somewhat extreme emotions: happiness and anger. We largely avoid the emotional space between them—where feelings like grief, loss, sadness, and anxiety reside—because we perceive these feelings as liabilities, as inconvenient or somehow at odds with idealistic notions of what a successful life should look like. At best, we lack tools to navigate this gray area. At worst, though, we fear others may perceive our emotional vulnerability as weakness, so we retreat into anger or happiness. These feel less threatening and require less vulnerability, mostly because neither emotion requires us to examine ourselves very deeply. When we express anger, for instance, we signal to others that the problem isn't our fault but someone else's. Anger can also give us a profound sense of self-righteousness, allowing us to feel powerful and in control of the situation. Anger is becoming increasingly socially acceptable—it's almost come to be a virtue rather than a vice. Indeed, anger and happiness are likely the most frequently expressed emotions on social media. Our news feeds are filled with either uninhibited boasts of happiness or toxic rants of perceived injustices.

Our habit of avoiding the emotional space between perceived happiness and anger is a tendency, which has developed over generations, of a lifestyle that increasingly values material accomplishment, status, and possessions at the expense of a healthy inner life. It's become clear that this does not work. For years the mental health crisis has been intensifying around the world. Whether misery itself has increased or people are just finding more visible ways to act out a misery that has always been there, avoiding our emotions and inner life has cost us dearly, both on an individual and societal level.

We have forgotten that we can find depth of heart and character in the emotional space between happiness and anger. Working through the nuances of that emotional gray area—even when our society deems this healing work inconvenient or unproductive—allows us to gain greater insight, self-awareness, empathy, compassion, sensitivity, patience, and richness of feeling. Turning to face and even embrace the more painful aspects of our emotional world makes us stronger and unearths the treasures of wisdom and resilience. Indeed, it is in this emotional space that we find ourselves, because here we stop avoiding the larger dimensions of our inner world. After all, how can we maintain a strong sense of self when we avoid so much of our emotional world, or it is even unknown to us? Indeed, venturing into the more painful aspects of ourselves—the parts our society does not glorify or esteem—is a plunge, one that profoundly rejects the superficial qualities our society idealizes. Yet there is no easier path toward becoming our true selves than choosing to dive into the deeper aspects of ourselves.

The Purpose of Healing Work

After finishing my first book, *Healing Your Wounded Soul: Growing from Pain to Peace*, it became clear to me that people needed something more to guide them toward transformation of mind and soul. That book introduced readers to the basic process of healing, drawing attention to how past hurts affect us in the present and how this can hinder our spiritual life if we leave them unresolved. Just as the lighthouse on the book's cover sent a beam of light into the night sky, *Healing Your Wounded Soul* sought to illumine darker aspects of our inner life that many of us find easier to avoid. While remaining blind to our inner pain can be perilous, the light of healing—like that of a lighthouse—leads us safely back to the shore of ourselves and helps us avoid emotional and spiritual shipwrecks along the way. It seems that the first book helped many readers realize their own unresolved pain and awoke within them a desire for resolution. For some, this awakening was enough to lessen the effects of their wounds and enable them to find some measure of healing. For others, however, the healing process remained abstract, the starting point elusive. *Where do I begin my healing journey? they wondered. How do I actually do this?*

Bearing this in mind, *Healing Work* is essentially a how-to guide to help readers locate the starting point in their own healing process and gain confidence in responding to the ebbs and flows, successes and setbacks, of the healing journey. I invite those familiar with my first book to use this one as a kind of companion edition, a collection of tools to aid them in bringing about long-term resolution and resilience.

But *Healing Work* is more than a sequel. It can also be read as a stand-alone, practical guide to healing, one that is particularly intended for people suffering from persistent, deeply rooted emotional wounds and for those who seek to help them. It's worth noting, too, that this book was written for individuals who are unable or unwilling to participate in counseling. Many feel reticent to seek professional help, perhaps because they have been disappointed with psychotherapy in the past or because of personal convictions. (In the Orthodox world, for example, some prefer to rely on their spiritual father to guide them through the healing process.) Others wish they could see a counselor but lack access to mental health care services or geographical proximity to them. Although virtual therapy is becoming more commonplace, many feel uncomfortable sharing their sensitive inner wounds through screens rather than in face-to-face conversation. *Healing Work* suits people who cannot or choose not to work with a counselor, whatever the reason.

Regardless of who picks up *Healing Work* and why they decide to read it, however, the goal is the same. As ambitious as it might sound, this book is about helping people learn how to make their healing journey shorter. It's tragic that so many get stuck in distressing emotional patterns for years or even decades, often because they simply don't know how to identify why they are suffering. They spend precious time, money, and energy scrambling to resolve isolated symptoms, never gaining awareness of their root cause(s). This doesn't have to happen. We can work to reduce unnecessary emotional suffering by learning to identify what we need to focus on and by developing skills to navigate the emotional space between the extremes of anger and happiness. In doing so, we can shorten the amount of time we struggle to move forward in our healing work.

How to Read This Book

It is not wholly necessary to navigate this book sequentially. The chapters do not lay out the healing process in exact chronological order because everyone's journey is unique. Some may benefit from reading chapter by chapter, while others may find themselves gravitating toward material in later chapters first as they begin their healing work. More important than what order readers move through this book is that they do so in a way that works for them and that they take the time to reflect on the content and integrate what they learn with their own experiences.

That said, readers will find it helpful to have a general overview of the material in mind. *Healing Work* starts with the life story. Readers will learn to identify the starting point in their healing journey by learning to tell their story through creating a narrative of their lives and their pain (see Chapter 1). Chapter 2 builds on this and asks how we can use the life story to gain insight about our lives and struggles. Chapter 3 aims to help readers make sense of struggles in their lives that are uniquely activated by the passage of time and the onset of certain life stages, like adulthood or retirement. Throughout the healing journey, it's important to step back and see the big picture of what we are facing. Chapter 4 helps us do that essential work of taking stock and understanding context. Otherwise, we easily fall into the trap of focusing on individual struggles without understanding how they fit within the whole of our lives. Until we learn to see these issues in context, our attempts to resolve them will be like pulling weeds out of a garden yet leaving their roots intact—our struggles may become less visible for a time, but they'll soon be back. We may also have learned unhealthy and unreasonable roles in the past that we play in the present. It's vital that we begin to step out of these roles and relinquish their unreasonable objectives.

Chapter 5 focuses on specific tools and approaches to help us heal through identifying and resolving deep-seated negative beliefs. The field of cognitive behavioral therapy (CBT) gives us a wonderful and faith-friendly toolbox full of techniques that allow us to see and reshape harmful beliefs, attitudes, and behaviors that have formed as a result of our experiences. This book will teach the reader how to apply these skills to their life and how to weave them into their spiritual life. Yet CBT does not resolve all wounds, particularly those that result from deep life disappointments, griefs, and traumas. Chapter 6 examines this reality, in particular the way they injure the brain and what strategies we can use to undo that damage according to current research.

Finally, Chapter 7 steps back and reflects on the healing path as a whole, revisiting certain general pitfalls and demonstrating how to continue making progress over the long term.

Why Give Humanity a Second Chance?

We are interconnected with one another; thus, nearly all our painful experiences involve another human being. As a result, we often emerge from these experiences with a damaged perception of humanity. One acutely painful experience has the ability to move to the forefront of all our experiences with humanity, causing our memories of positive interactions with others to fade. We begin to see life through the lens of this painful experience, and all of humanity can become suspect and no longer trustworthy. When this happens, we distance ourselves from others and become too quick to engage in defensive behavior—whether that's avoidance, or responding to others as though they had participated in our past unresolved experience.

Perhaps the most significant and beautiful outcome of the healing work is that we learn to give humanity a second chance. We need others, and we cannot complete our healing work by detouring them. As we heal, and decrease avoidance and protective behaviors, we will have new, positive experiences that gradually move to the forefront of our memories. The painful experiences that so dominated our lives take their place in the past and are put to rest. Indeed, humanity has the power to harm and to heal. The healing work helps us to be at peace with this paradox. By giving humanity a second chance, we get to experience its healing power.

Healing Work as Ascetical Work

It bears reminding that this healing work is ascetical. It is part of our spiritual life, not separate from it. When we commit to this healing work, we have the conviction that under no circumstances will we tolerate any obstacle standing between ourselves, God, and our neighbor. As readily as we begin to see the wounded aspects of ourselves, we will set upon the work of discovering their origins and identifying what we need to do to resolve them and free ourselves from their negative effects. It involves a grit and determination to leave no stone unturned in our inner world so that we might labor spiritually most efficiently in this limited time God has given us.

The type of emotional experiences we have had will largely

determine what we need to do to find resolution and relief. There is no one-size-fits-all approach to resolving our painful experiences. For some of us, particularly if our experiences were profoundly painful, we might only need insight, processing, and getting some emotion up and out. We might find it enough to troubleshoot troublesome situations—such as difficult social interactions—by learning to identify our triggers, meanings assigned, and beliefs formed, and how to revise them and to know their origins. For some of us, it may be as simple as learning how not to feel threatened by our negative emotions and instead how to sit with them. For many, it is the fear of our emotions, of feeling certain things, which causes so many of our most troublesome symptoms.

Where Healing Work Begins

This book is built on the premise that true and total healing can occur. Being a wounded soul does not have to be a permanent or perpetual state. It isn't, or at least need not be, our lifelong identity. Certain therapeutic and support group settings operate on the assumption that once a wounded soul, always a wounded soul—that if a person has need of therapeutic intervention and support services, they will forever need them to stay afloat emotionally. This view offers little hope that we can find full and total healing from past experiences.

Regardless of how prominent this assumption is, we could also argue that our minds and souls are capable of complete, and in some sense permanent, healing. Advancements and discoveries

16

in therapy research, specifically in our understanding of how painful experiences affect the brain, have brought about new areas of exploration and approaches to therapy. These emerging strategies can help the brain relearn how to respond, relate, perceive, and feel. In essence, we are finding ways to help our minds heal from injury—not physical injuries, but deep emotional and spiritual ones.

In a sense, at least for the purposes of this book, it doesn't matter what kind of injury, whether it's diagnosed trauma or simply a painful sense of disappointment and regret in life. This book will speak to all profoundly painful events we can experience. An experience does not have to be traumatic in a clinical sense to leave a mark on us. Depending on our life experiences, certain chapters of this book might resonate more than others. However, the knowledge that can be gained from each chapter will be universally useful to all, regardless of the unique history of their woundedness. And even if we have not suffered any profoundly painful experiences that have left a mark, undoubtedly we know others who have.

This book starts from the premise that we—indeed, humanity as a whole—have all suffered because of events that should not have happened. Why is this important to clarify in a book about healing? Because sometimes in our effort to make sense of the pain in our lives and the life of the world, we buy into the assumption that if something "bad" occurs, it was meant to happen. We should accept it and move on. Yet this is a form of avoidance, a way to turn away from the complexity and reality of the free will of ourselves and others. Instead, we must exercise great caution when asserting that anything resulting from these free choices was meant to happen. When we use our free will to engage in behavior that harms others, we cannot justify it as something that was "supposed to" happen that way. Such excuses could do great harm to others, not to mention to ourselves. Further, they lead to the belief that those who suffer—which sometimes includes ourselves—somehow deserve what they experience. In the end, these assumptions undermine trust in God and in others, and they inflict people with a terrible sense of shame.

There is another way beyond these simplistic assumptions that we will always be wounded and that the bad things are meant to happen. When we start to step back to see the larger picture of our lives, when we start encountering new experiences that result from transforming the ways we relate with ourselves, others, and our surroundings, then we begin to feel as though we had never suffered the painful experiences. We reach a place where memories learn to be past memories, where previous emotional triggers no longer trigger us. We learn to relate with ourselves and our external world as if we had not suffered those past experiences. It's true that we will always have memories of the painful experiences we've endured, but when we engage in healing work, they have a chance to fade and lose their power over us. In short, we get to keep the good and let go of the bad. Even if our wounds are deep, once we encounter healing, we get to keep the wisdom and humility we gained from working through those painful experiences while also letting go of the fear, pain, and shame that once held us captive.

Healing Work as Heroic Work

Shame is almost always the debilitating companion of painful experiences. When we suffer from shame, we often go through life feeling forever associated with the painful or traumatic experience. It becomes part of us, woven into the very fabric of our being, and it can feel like a garment or stigma that we bear but wish we did not. However, is this the fate we must resign ourselves to if we have suffered painful experiences? It is not. It does not need to become our legacy. There is indeed a much better legacy within our reach. When we experience shame, we perceive ourselves in a distorted way, so we will need a new way to perceive ourselves. We can learn to replace our debilitating shame with something far more realistic, and that is heroism: we embrace the identity of a hero.

Healing from trauma is a heroic task. Combat veterans often convert their service and experience into something quite the opposite of shame, and thus they can readily be acknowledged as heroes. So can any survivor of trauma. What might have once been a source of pain and shame becomes a source of pride and a sense of honor. We often see veterans express this by wearing hats that detail their service, or ribbons, or even medals showing they were in combat. Indeed, we call them heroes and we thank them for their service. Would we ever state that a combat veteran should feel shame when they have healed from their experiences, raised a healthy family, bore their pain without taking it out on their family or others, and become a better person? We would not.

However, for those who have suffered painful experiences outside of combat, there will be no ceremony, no medals, no formal recognition—at least not in this life. For some of us, though, our children may one day, either while we are still alive in this world or after we are gone, discover the pain we had to bear and marvel that they never bore the brunt of it because of our love, faith, and conviction. This knowledge would also reveal that their parent succeeded in the epic feat of bearing and resolving the family pain without it reaching their children. To bear pain and not allow it to affect others negatively is heroic. Learning to thrive, despite having our proverbial wings clipped through witnessing or experiencing traumatic situations, is indeed heroic, and a service to humanity. Can there be any greater form of heroism?

May readers find themselves on the path to heroism—a heroism tempered with humility—that is the gift of the healing work.

CHAPTER 1

Finding Our Starting Point
Creating Our Narrative

A FTER WE REALIZE AND ACCEPT that we are ready to address the unresolved in our life, we begin by telling our story. For some of us, this task might seem easy, yet for others it is not. However, whether we can readily formulate and tell our life story or whether we must exert more effort to do so, the benefits and objective are the same. When we tell our story, we create the narrative of our life. For many of us, this narrative can be the outline of our healing process. It provides a general chronological map we will follow, and as we move through it, it reveals the areas we need to address.

What Is a Life Story?

In its most basic form, a life story is our way of answering the existential questions *where am I in my life, and how did I end up in this place?* A life story is more than a resume; it consists not simply of milestones, accomplishments, important dates, or places we've lived. It is our *story*—our understanding of the road we have traveled, of how we became who we are today. It starts with our earliest memories and with childhood. It narrates what our home environment and relationships with our parents and siblings were like. It shares what kind of child and teen we were and what social relationships were important to us when we were growing up. A life story also includes any significant events we feel have affected us emotionally or even developmentally—strained relationships with family members, for example. We weave into our story, too, whatever insight we have gained about the ways these experiences have changed us.

What exactly does the narrative look like? What form should it take? There is no right answer. When we begin to create our narrative, we can use any format we choose. Some may gravitate toward a linear timeline with notes and insights (see Appendix A, page 158, for an example). Others choose to write out their story in paragraph form (see Appendix B, page 160). If we choose to document our life story in one of these written forms, doing so in a journal devoted to the purpose is ideal. It should have enough space not only for your life story but for further reflection on different aspects of it. (More will be said about this later in this chapter.)

Another option is to record the narrative in audio format. Some people find processing information aloud more helpful, and they tend to find it easier and more enjoyable to play back and hear their narrative rather than read it on a page. An added benefit here is that we have the option to hear our own voice tell our story, which can be a powerful, insight-generating tool when we answer questions like: *How did I feel when I heard my own voice tell my life story?* and *What did I learn from how I sounded?* We might even decide to ask another trusted and sensitive person to listen to the recording and give us feedback. Their impressions or empathy could provide a sense of connection or even dismantle certain emotional roadblocks.

Finally, we can use some combination of all three formats. For example, we could start with making a basic timeline, then gradually fill it in until it reads like a story, then record and listen to ourselves telling that story.

However we choose to document our life story, it is crucial we begin by stepping back and shifting our perspective enough so that we start to see our lives in a more reflective way. Life has a way of throwing events and experiences at us faster than we can process them, and it doesn't take many years before we begin to feel like our life is a ball of tangled experiences. Some of these experiences might be significant, and we thought we had processed them or assumed we'd resolved them, but they still have loose ends attached. When we live our life without taking time to form and know our narrative—our life story—we can easily begin to feel out of control and as if we lack direction. Formulating the narrative of our life involves pausing time, stepping back, and seeing the proverbial forest for the trees. The forest, of course, is our overall life, and the trees are the many experiences that affect us.

The healing work of formulating our life story requires two different kinds of stepping back. There is, first, an initial stepping back. For this, we have to hit pause on our preoccupation with our present circumstances and work to perceive our experiences as a whole. Only then can we tell our life story. However, after we do this and begin to review that narrative, we have to step back in a second way to help ourselves glean further insight and perspective (see Chapters 3 and 4).

Why Create a Life Story?

There are many benefits to strengthening awareness of our life story and formulating it as a narrative. Not only does the narrative alleviate the feeling that our lives are somehow chaotic or unmanageable, it also helps us feel more grounded and less out of control. We acquire a greater sense of knowing where we are, and we are better able to plot our course moving forward. We become more aware of the chronological order of our experiences. We are able to plot the jumbled ball of our life experiences on the timeline of our life in this world. Discerning the sequence of events we've experienced evokes a sense of meaning and organization in a life that may have previously seemed disordered and confusing. When we pause, step back, and recognize the larger picture, we clarify what has happened, what we have accomplished, and what yet needs to be done.

Writing a life story is the starting point of our healing work and will reveal much about the perceptions we have of ourselves and lives thus far. It will also uncover some of the ways we've come to relate to ourselves and how we explain certain events. *What meaning(s) have I assigned to what happened to me?* is as important a question as *What happened to me?* What story have I told about the more painful events of my life? What do I believe these experiences *mean* about me as a person? How we answer these questions has a massive impact on our lives. It

24

profoundly affects our relationship with others, with God, and with ourselves.

We would do well to remember also that our own life story is made up of many other life stories: all those of our kin who came before us. As a companion exercise to writing our own life story or narrative, it may be helpful for us to review the life stories of those who came before us such as our parents, grandparents, and even great-grandparents. We have been affected by their life experiences in some way, whether they influenced us through their parenting or through epigenetics. Indeed, the life story of great-grandparents affected our grandparents, which affected our parents, which in turn affected us.

Common Challenges with Creating a Life Narrative

While putting words to our life journey can bring relief for some, many of us may recoil in horror or grief when confronted with what we have experienced so far. It isn't easy to face the reality of our lives, especially if we have been in the habit of avoidance and of pushing memories as far as possible from our conscious minds. In the case of avoidance, we may already know on some level how we feel about the life we have lived—we just resist facing those feelings. If we have been pushing our memories away, though, we might just be beginning to process the emotions associated with our life experiences.

Another challenge occurs when, as we set out to create our narrative, we struggle to recall certain life events. Fortunately, it's not necessary to remember every detail of the past to formulate our story. We can work with what we do remember, knowing there will be gaps or blank spots where we sense something happened but can't quite remember what. Some peoples' narratives will be complete and cohesive, yet other narratives will look more like Swiss cheese. Even then, however, it is still a narrative and can help reveal the areas we need to address.

Beginning to Work with Our Narrative

What should we do with our life story once we finish creating it? Before we answer this question, it's important to note that our narrative is a work in progress—we are free to revise or add to it as we gain greater insight and self-awareness throughout the healing process. And although "finishing" the narrative is only part of the journey, most of us will derive at least some benefit simply from the process of creating it. It helps us gain a sense of mastery over previous experiences that we had not fully processed. Also, for some time our mind has probably wanted to release some of what we included in our narrative.

After finishing the initial version of our life story, some of us will need to take a break for several days or weeks before proceeding to the next step of reflecting on it. If this is the first time we are really beginning to address the pockets of pain within us, creating our life story may leave us feeling emotionally tender or raw. This may also become an opportunity to grieve, which is usually a healthy sign that we have started to face reality and accept our life as it truly is—and as it truly was.

Once we have taken whatever time we need to regain a feeling of equilibrium, we are ready to step back and start reviewing and reflecting on our narrative. This is where recording our life story in a journal—as recommended earlier in this chapter—becomes useful, at least for those who choose to craft their narrative in written form. A journal can serve as a container not only for the narrative itself but for our ongoing reflections regarding it. (Those who record their narrative in some other format will simply want to make sure they store the narrative and subsequent reflections in a way they can easily organize, access, and retrieve.) If we use a journal, our narrative should be in the opening pages. It's a good idea to leave several blank pages after that for any revisions or additions we may wish to make in the future.

Identifying the Parts of Our Story
Where We Desire Healing and Resolution

We will reserve the rest of our journal for what we glean from our life story. What did we learn from it? What do we need to resolve? What changes do we want that resolution to create in our present life? Here are some basic items a person might take note of as they review their life story:

» I want to resolve the past, so I can better trust the present.

» I want to complete the unresolved grief over the sad events of my childhood, so I can be more joyful in the present.

» I want to more fully process that past frightening experience, so I am not so anxious in the present.

These examples are fairly general, and although they lack detail, they signify some important first steps toward learning to identify areas where we desire resolution and healing. Over time, though, and as we gain more insight throughout our healing journey, we will hopefully be able to name these areas with greater specificity:

» I want to work through, process, and grieve unfair roles and positions I was put in as a child, so I'm not always trying to control the uncontrollable as an adult.

» I want to more fully process and heal from the powerlessness I experienced as a child, in order to be more at peace with not having control in my present life.

» I want to heal more from the uncertainty and unpredictability of my earlier life, so I can better tolerate uncertainty in the present.

» I want to heal from an abusive relationship that destroyed my ability to trust, so I can learn to trust others again.

These examples give an idea of how we can develop and frame goals as we create our narrative and become more familiar with it.

Seven Questions to Ask When Reflecting on Our Life Story

Arriving at goals and insights like those above may prove difficult. Some may wish to do more reflecting after identifying some initial goals. In many ways, we can use the narrative we have shaped as a diagnostic tool to help us identify the sources of the struggles that have followed us throughout our lives. These seven points of inquiry help us sharpen our understanding of our life story and reveal areas where we need healing:

1. What theme(s) connects both my present and past life?

2. Are there any elements from my past, even those I assumed I had put behind me, that reappear in the present?

3. How might I be reenacting past roles and dynamics in my present relationships?

4. To what extent have I sought avoidance in the present so that I don't have to re-experience events from the past?

5. To what extent, and in what ways, do previous experiences remain an issue for me, even if I have been telling myself that the past is over?

6. Are there roles I learned in the past that I still try to fulfill in the present, even if they are not healthy for me?

7. How much of my life have I spent trying to prove something? For example, do I try to convince myself or others that certain things I was made to believe about myself in my early life are not true?

Facing the Painful Elements of Our Life Story

We may become emotional when we review our narrative. This is normal, healthy, and often beneficial. Our life story could lead us to a place of gratitude, but it could also prompt a deep pang of regret. However, even when we're faced with regret, we can turn that regret into gratitude when we use it to make amends with others. Although realizing the past has taken a toll on our present life and relationships can be difficult, it can also illuminate the steps of healing we need to take. It can be an opportunity for us to become more aware of our negative behavior and to change. It can also help us recognize the things and people we have neglected and to seek forgiveness. So long as we have these realizations while we are still in this world, we have the time and opportunity to change—it's never too late. The reality is that no one's story is perfect, nor without actions that have hurt others.

Likewise, creating our narrative can be an opportunity for others when we bring to their attention something hurtful that they did. They have to respond to this encounter. Yes, they might respond positively or negatively. Nevertheless, they have the opportunity to respond well, to obtain forgiveness, and to change. This can happen when we face parts of our story where we ourselves have been hurt.

Telling our story highlights the way others have affected us, whether positively or negatively. To be clear, the telling of our story doesn't create such problems or wounds—it doesn't introduce a new reality that was not already there. It simply causes us to face our life story and raises awareness of experiences we may have suppressed, minimized, or avoided. When this happens, namely, when we spend years burying recognition of an unhealthy role someone played in our lives, there is a good chance we have paid the price for it in the form of self-blame, shame, and feelings of inadequacy.

So often it is easier to blame ourselves rather than the one actually at fault. It's also safer to blame ourselves—or at least, it feels that way—because acknowledging the unhealthy role someone played in our lives could mean confrontation or setting boundaries that could lead to conflict. However, self-blame is a form of self-injury, albeit one that is not our fault. Sometimes we embrace the belief that it is easier and less risky to just take the blame. However, this does not work, for while taking the blame might enable us to avoid conflict or confrontation with another, we sentence ourselves to a life of shame and self-loathing that paralyzes us. Our life story will likely bring a spotlight to this phenomenon so we can see it on the conscious level. This does not mean that telling our life story is a threat to our relationships. It means we might need to make adjustments and give voice to how others have contributed to our life story, whether for good or for ill.

Often, the ones who were responsible for a painful experience are still in our lives. Discerning what to do with this realization can be challenging—we might not know how to feel, and that is normal. We might find ourselves vacillating between anger and guilt—anger that we were mistreated and guilt that it happened in the first place. Or perhaps we feel angry because we are just now seeing the mistreatment in a new way, or we experience guilt because of how angry we feel. Some have difficulty acknowledging that they experienced anything negative from core relationships in their lives: for example, their parents.

We often tend toward an all-or-nothing understanding of parental relationships. We worry that if we acknowledge anything negative a parent (or any significant other) did to us, we are somehow slandering their legacy, are ungrateful, or are saying they are "bad parents." However, the truth is often in the gray. If indeed our struggles and negative beliefs are tied to our family of origin, it doesn't mean our parents or family were "bad." Negative traits can coexist alongside positive ones in a person or within relationship systems. Even if our parents were often well-intentioned, no one is perfect. We can come to terms with the negative ways they have affected us while still loving them and keeping the relationship intact. We can recognize the unhealthy ways we avoid acknowledging the weaknesses in how we were parented. To acknowledge these things, and to understand that we might have suffered due to family dynamics and how we were treated growing up, does not mean we are being a bad child. It means we are trying to heal ourselves, so we can be our true selves and pass on better parenting to our children. It also serves to preserve the relationship with our parents in the long term. The misdeeds of others will not cease to exist simply because we avoid or ignore them. They will stay with us, and them. And in fact, telling our life story might even contribute to the betterment and salvation of the other.

Self-Compassion: Treating Ourselves as Christ Would

Among the most crucial abilities we need as we explore our narrative is self-compassion and mercy. Many people struggle to accept this concept of self-compassion and the truth that it is okay to be merciful with ourselves. Some might equate self-compassion with self-indulgence and deem it spiritually dangerous. Yet it's okay, even vital, to show mercy to ourselves.

Self-compassion doesn't mean we don't challenge ourselves, nor does it give us permission to act out in spiritually unhealthy ways. Instead, self-compassion is important for long-term spiritual balance and growth. When we exercise self-compassion, we in essence treat ourselves as Christ would treat us, acknowledging the reality that although we have lived imperfect lives, we ought not condemn ourselves with self-blame, loathing, and corrosive shame. Self-compassion is acceptance followed by a strong desire and a yearning to heal that which is broken and fallen within us. When we do not exercise self-compassion, shame and negative ways of relating to ourselves and others soon follow, which will stifle rather than nourish our spiritual growth. These tendencies can also prevent us from acknowledging key parts of our life story.

We sometimes doubt our experiences or their significance, and this is another area where learning to be self-compassionate is essential. To tell our narrative means it's okay to face the reality that painful things have happened to us. This kind of realization is not self-pity—we are not playing the victim. If we cannot validate and take ownership of our own experiences, we cannot begin the healing process. When we are short on self-compassion, we tend to devalue ourselves and our life experiences. We might overlook rather painful ways people have hurt us because "others have it much worse." Even more painful, if we blame ourselves for something we weren't responsible for, we might regard our painful experience as a deserved punishment rather than as something we need to acknowledge and heal. We can go through our whole life living with a life sentence for a crime we never committed.

Yet for some of us, when we acknowledge we were the victim and that what happened to us was traumatic or just painful, we then worry what that means about us. In other words, we may resist validating our life experiences, for that means we were powerless and weak. This can lead to a great deal of shame that we will need to work through. The ability to show mercy to ourselves is one of the most critical abilities we need in order to create our narrative and in the overall healing process.

CHAPTER 2

Wielding the Power of Insight

H EALING WORK IS NOT UNLIKE watching a line of dominoes in action. The different aspects of areas we need healing for are often interlocked. Just as no domino can fall unless the one before it does, we can't settle certain issues of our healing until we resolve others first. Sometimes the dominoes simply stop falling—they are too crowded or far apart and lose momentum until another force intervenes to continue the process. In our own journey, too, there may be times when, no matter how hard we work or how much we desire to push through the process, we encounter a pause or plateau in our growth. These pauses provide opportunities for us to take a break and spend time inhabiting the new place we've been able to reach. It's almost as though our mind grants us time to adjust to new ways of perceiving or relating to our new space before it pushes us on to resolve the next issue. These temporary lulls are not departures from the healing process but are integral to it—they afford us a chance to regroup, rest, and give thanks before continuing our ascent.

Eventually, though, the break will come to an end and the difficult journey will continue. What drives the momentum to get moving again can seem like mystery. A triggering experience or interaction may cause us to suddenly and inexplicably see things that were not evident before. What is often happening, however, is that the healing work we've been doing has borne new insight, a fresh new lens through which we can see and make better sense of our experiences. This new way of seeing allows us to perceive aspects of ourselves we didn't recognize before, which in turn leads us to the next insight—and the line of dominoes continues to topple.

Insight, then, is one of the most vital tools to cultivate on the path to resolution. We can understand insight as the capacity to gain an accurate and deep, intuitive understanding of a person or thing. It's essentially the ability to look within ourselves and objectively observe our cognitive and emotional processes.

To visualize how insight occurs, we can think of some-one sitting on the bank of a stream and observing the flowing water. As they keep their gaze steady, they can train their eyes to see through the water to the bottom of the riverbed. At times, the water is murky and they can't see through it, but they keep watching—with patience, the water eventually runs clear. Sometimes this clarity is short-lived, and then the person catches only a glimpse of what lies underneath before the mud and murk return. So it is with us when we employ the skill of insight. Sometimes when we attempt to look within, we know something is there, but we can't quite get at it. But much like the person observing the stream, with time and patience, we will achieve those moments where we suddenly catch sight of what we've been looking for. Perhaps the insight is realizing what's really bothering us about a particular situation, for example, or why we're feeling a certain way, or what meaning we've been assigning to a distressing event.

Insight as a Process

It's important to note at the outset that insight alone will not heal us. It does help and can bring us great relief, but ultimately its purpose is to lead us deeper into the experiential and emotional process of healing, which likewise allows us to transform how we perceive and relate to the various areas of our lives. Nevertheless, insight is liberating. It creates a sense of unlocking or solving a long-elusive mystery. Individual insights often prompt us to break through what's blocking our path and take the next step in healing.

Yet this whole process—the unfolding of insight, and the healing process in general—is not necessarily endless. Eventually, there may come a time when an insight brings us to the final stage of healing from a particular issue. In other words, we reach a point where we are one insight away from getting the emotion or distress or painful pattern up and out of us. We can resolve painful experiences to the point where it is as though they did not occur. Even better, we can heal in such a way that we no longer live according to the pain of a past experience, but we still get to keep the wisdom and resilience we gained from it. Armed with new knowledge gained from insight, we can change how we respond to situations, ourselves, people, and God.

What does this process look like in an everyday context? Let's say someone gains the insight—or realization—that they have been engaging in reenactments. A reenactment occurs when we unconsciously recreate similar relationship patterns in our present life as a way of coping with painful ones from the past. For example, if we suffered the pain of rejection early in life, in our present, we may reject others before they reject us, as a way to protect ourselves. This can be the result of being hypervigilant for any signs of rejection by others. By engaging in defensive or hypersensitive reactions to others, we create the very scenario we are trying to protect ourselves from. Once we gain insight into these reenactments and can clearly recognize them in our life, we then start changing our responses and reactions to others. This, then, creates new experiences and allows us a sense of safety that we have not experienced before. We no longer must expend extra energy to defend ourselves and keep ourselves safe; this allows us to become aware of the next layer of healing work. Once we feel safe and no longer distracted by a defensive disposition, we suddenly become aware of the deeper issue: that we were not protected when we were younger during a particularly painful experience. This insight taps into a pocket of unresolved grief over a basic unmet need. We are now able to express grief that should have occurred many years ago but never did. The mind is ready to release this hidden wound and pain now that certain obstacles or layers have been removed.

We also see in this example how insight helps unlock emotions from past painful events that we've suppressed or bottled up. Buried emotions are like pockets or reservoirs trapped beneath the surface of our conscious mind. These hidden chambers of emotion contain feelings we needed to feel at the time an event occurred (or in its immediate aftermath) but never did. No matter how much time or distance we try to put between us and the event, those emotions will stay frozen in their little compartments until we can get them up, out, and released. When we seek and engage insight, we essentially dig through the layers of the subconscious and unconscious mind until we hit one of these pockets of buried emotion. This allows for a cathartic and healing emotional release. Such moments can grant immense relief in themselves. When we connect the dots and comprehend why something has been bothering us so much, we find greater peace. It is as though our mind and heart sigh with relief that we have finally let out a deeply held secret.

Reasons We Avoid Developing Insight

There are many obstacles that keep us from leaning into insight, some of them internal (in the form of fears, for example) and others external (busy schedules that allow for little time to reflect). Let's begin by examining a few of the internal hurdles. First, striving to become more insightful is a process that requires trust, which we don't always find easy. Many fear what lies within and therefore find it difficult to trust that moments of insight will bring relief rather than overwhelm. While some are eager to dig into healing work, driven by an intense desire to feel better, others are more cautious to start excavating, even if they know they need to do it.

Those who identify with the latter may find it helpful to recognize that by the time we are ready to address something difficult from the past, we have already come a long way. We have made it to the battlefield, and this is an achievement in itself. It's normal to have trepidation about the struggle we perceive ahead. After all, healing work is an ascetical arena. While it will ultimately strengthen us spiritually and emotionally, first we will have to wage battle against fear, pride, ego, and distorted perceptions of ourselves and others. We can ask God for courage in our battle for resolution. Courage is defined as the ability to do something frightening or to display strength in the face of pain or grief. Courage does not mean the absence of fear but an ability to still function and push forward even though we might be afraid. As we wield insight and courageously engage the unresolved, we will gain virtues that will benefit all other areas of our lives—wisdom, easier access to humility, peace, self-control, patience, and depth of heart. Indeed, knowing that we can gain these traits through our own healing work can powerfully motivate us to move forward and engage the process.

A second internal obstacle to insight is not fear but rather a kind of stubbornness. If we happen to struggle acutely with pride or ego in our spiritual lives, the insight we gain may seem inconvenient or uncomfortable, especially if it conflicts with how we perceive ourselves. The incongruence between the perception we had of ourselves and the new understanding of ourselves we gained through insight can be difficult to accept. Resisting insight is often a deliberate and willful act, a preference for blindness rather than for facing reality and accepting the need for change. Yet this kind of choice will stifle our healing. We can counter this obstacle with humility, which goes hand in hand with insight. Humility allows us to overcome incongruence. It is like an anesthesia that allows us to bear the pain of insights into ourselves that contradict our usual self-perception. It enables us to sit in the space of evolving self-awareness, to take it all in, and plot what we need to do next.

Yes, insight may force us to feel and confront certain negative emotions, which can be frightening. But our feelings are simply our feelings; they can't hurt us. It's our *perception* of our feelings that can hurt and overwhelm us. As will become clearer throughout this book, if we can simply be willing to wade into the emotions that come up and push through them, we will find that they are temporary. They will be resolved once we accomplish the work that we need to do.

The tendency to resist insight because of our ego or out of stubbornness is like when someone comes to a large body of water and, although passing through it would be most efficient, they search for a way around it. Even though the journey of healing is murky, latent with perceived uncertainty, and tends to get things wetter and messier along the way, once we pass through the deep work, we will have gained courage and the satisfaction from having done so. Giving in to the temptation to find a detour around the work—just like the traveler who tried to find a route around the water—will mean a longer, and perhaps endless, journey. We can spend years trying to get around healing work, perhaps comforting ourselves with fantasies of shortcuts and detours. Some, indeed, spend a lifetime stuck in this mode, never really progressing. If we want to move forward in our journey, however, and eventually reach our destination, we will need to accept that there are no ways around the deep waters of pain—we will need to wade through them.

Once we begin the healing work and follow the way of insight, we will gain confidence in our ability to handle the emotions that arise. We learn that not only do they not cause damage to us, but they actually, in the long run, make us feel better. It's paradoxical but often true: the more we feel and sit with difficult emotions, the more they weaken and dissipate. We can learn to trust that process as well.

Let us turn now to examine an external obstacle to pursuing insight: busyness. Our lifestyle today does not lend itself to being and becoming insightful. We move through our days at a frenetic pace. The many activities and tasks we pack into our lives throw experiences at us faster than we can process. At any given time, our plates are so full that when life sends us an unexpected trial, we become easily overwhelmed, if we are not already. Our time allows us little opportunity to reflect, much less engage in deep introspection. Indeed, without realizing it, we become accustomed to resisting depth in our thoughts and inner life. We get used to just staying on the surface of our awareness without ever peeking underneath to make sure everything is in order, and making adjustments if needed. Our lifestyle today encourages avoidance. Many of us go morning till night without having much time to think or process our day. Before we know it, our mind becomes a place of jumbled and unsorted experiences. When we get swept up in that frenetic speed and pay little attention to what is going on within us, inevitably we start to feel out of control. Hitting the pause button, saying no to more activity, and taking time to unpack and make sense of a day that has just passed is one way we can regain control over the pace of life. One of the long-term gains of having an insightful mind is that we feel more grounded and at peace, since our inner world is seen rather than unseen, known rather than unknown. It is orderly, sorted through, and everything is in its proper place. This gives us a greater sense of confidence as we face each new day and helps us feel calmer during times when our schedule must be busier. To start getting a feel for how busyness, and the accompanying stress, is affecting your life right now, see Exercise 1: Assigning Percentages to Current Stressors, in Appendix C, page 166.

Stages of Insight

Many of us have a hard time identifying or assessing our ability to be insightful or to wield insight. There are four stages of insight that will help us make this assessment more easily and aid us in our ability to identify where we are and what direction we need to work toward.

Insight is not something we develop overnight—it's a learning process. Some of us may begin our healing journey with virtually no insight. This does not mean we are a bad or selfish person; rather, some of us just seem hardwired to stay on the surface of our consciousness and not go deeper. We may move through life exhibiting automatic reactions to situations without ever having any awareness of why we reacted a certain way or how it may have made other people feel.

Possessing minimal insight can be either a blessing or a handicap, depending upon our disposition of heart. Consider someone who is pure-hearted, kind, guileless, gentle, and loves others as freely as they breathe. Such a soul does not need insight; their automatic and most natural responses are all they need. On the other hand, for most of us, a lack of insight tends to be a detriment to our spiritual lives. We may struggle with impulsive reactions to people and situations in our lives. We may gravitate toward negative behaviors, finding it difficult to love, trust, and in general live as God meant for us to live. It's clear we need insight to help us break free from these struggles.

Sometimes when we are in this state, we are also more prone to certain defense mechanisms such as projections. On an unconscious level, we may be prone to make our struggles an issue for someone else, as if our struggles were somehow *their* struggles or issues. We may also be more prone to displacement of our feelings onto others, transferences, and even reenactments. This is because we go through life on autopilot. Insight gives us the ability to catch ourselves when we engage in these and other defenses. It also makes us aware of them, which provides us with an opportunity to change our behavior and even apologize when necessary. Such moments allow us to walk the situation backward to trace its origins.

The second stage of insight we might find ourselves in is one of sporadic insight. We have moments of significant realizations, but they are fleeting. They do not persist, and we don't act on them because we either get distracted, lack the will or motivation to follow through, or simply don't want to accept or face certain truths. In this stage, we get glimpses of what our life could potentially become. However, the moments of insight turn into lost opportunities.

The third stage of insight is characterized by moderate to considerable insight but the inability to act upon it. We might be aware of the faults, flaws, and behaviors we need to correct, but we haven't been able to do anything about it for years or even decades. Someone in this state might be able to observe their flaws or even articulate them out loud, for example, "I know I have a sharp tongue; I know I have a problem with how I speak to people," but they are frozen and unable to effect change in their lives. Often when we are in this state, we realize what we need to do, but we feel paralyzed and don't know how to proceed. Why this inertia? For some it could come from a lack of motivation or the sense that having to change for others is inconvenient. For obvious reasons, this is not healthy and is ultimately selfish. Yet others feel paralyzed because they just don't know where to begin. Finally, we might be stuck due to some other unresolved issue in our life that is blocking us. (On this note, to see how insight leads to resolution of unresolved pockets of emotion, see Figure 1: How Insight Leads to Resolution, in Appendix C, page 167.)

The fourth stage of insight occurs when we are readily able to gain it after some persistence and follow-through as we act upon what the insight revealed to us. There are few things more beautiful than a life such as this—a life transformed, of continuous renewal. Indeed, this is a universal, lifelong calling for all of us. We can arrive at a point where this process of gaining insight and acting upon it is perpetual. Participating in it becomes like breathing. We become like our own investigator who, at any given time, has a list of cases that need solving. In this instance, the cases we need to solve are the aspects of ourselves that we need to change and resolve but have so far been unable to change.

In the fourth stage of insight, we typically ask ourselves, "How do I feel when I realize I have ultimately been acting selfishly?" Hopefully, regret strikes us and we feel humbled when we have the insight, and that alone will motivate us to initiate change. In such instances, a great starting point is simply doing the opposite of the negative behavior. We will soon be amazed at how this impacts the other people in our lives. This, then, humbles us further, as we more deeply realize what we have deprived others of, and for so long. Indeed, these long-awaited changes may end with heartfelt apologies for the time that was wasted.

These four stages of insight are not necessarily linear. Each of us can find ourselves in any stage of awareness and insight at any given moment. Thankfully, we can progress through stages, gradually becoming more insightful. It needs to be said that insight alone is in vain if we do not act upon it. No matter how insightful and self-aware we are, if these qualities do not translate into change, or at least a vigorous and genuine effort to change, then they are in vain. However, not everyone gradually becomes more insightful as they move through their life in this world. An initial lack of insight makes obtaining insight more difficult. We can get trapped in a cycle or loop in which we never pause and look within, and therefore, we never gain insight. As a result, we can spend an entire lifetime at one stage of insight, never making any progress.

Still, even when we are not moving forward, this is not a hopeless cycle. There are ways for this loop or cycle to be disrupted. We may have a life experience that causes us to become thoughtful or introspective in a way we never have before. Or a certain life experience may force us, or at least pressure us, to come to terms with certain realities. Moments such as these can be opportunities for us to see things in ourselves and in our lives that we had not previously seen or allowed ourselves to see. The life experience could be a health event that potentially affects our mortality or changes our lifestyle, a loss of someone close to us, or the arrival of a certain stage of life. Also, repeated, negative interpersonal experiences can bring us to a point where we suddenly become introspective and begin looking within for answers. Another example is getting direct feedback from others, sometimes by being confronted in an intervention-like way, about our behaviors or how we have been treating others. For some, these occurrences can lead to powerful and dramatic changes. Yet others might have some brief awakening to insight which is only fleeting and soon forgotten. Worse yet, some of us may resist looking within and instead respond by lashing out, getting angry, and blaming others. However, it is the first outcome we seek, the outcome of the occurrence as a catalyst for powerful and dramatic change.

If we genuinely seek to heal, transform our lives, and live how God wants us to live, then once we experience insight, we will seek and crave more of it. Insight gives way to more insight. Once we become open to working on ourselves and we get a taste of insight, it is very hard to go back to being closed to it. It is like what happens when someone enjoys reading mystery novels or solving puzzles. Once they experience the gratification of solving a mystery or puzzle, they will likely adopt the activity as a hobby. Once we become open to realizing and accepting that we have work to do on ourselves, and once we become adept at digesting the medicine, so to speak, that does not always taste good, we tend to develop an aversion to living in ignorance. If you're ready to get a start on the process now, try Exercise 2: Connecting Events and Emotions, which you can find in Appendix C, page 168.

The Fruits of an Insightful Mind and Heart

One final gift that insight brings about in our lives is depth of heart, a quality that can be hard to find in today's world. Depth of heart is the capacity to feel and think deeply. One who has depth of heart is often also tenderhearted, capable of demonstrating great compassion, and able to express a deep love. As we gain insight and improve our ability to think deeply, our minds and hearts have more inner space to explore. We can go to greater depths and become capable of greater exploration. As a result, we end up feeling more because we realize more. And then we can give others more in terms of relating with them better, showing empathy, listening better, displaying more patience, and even giving advice. Our overall life experiences become deeper, which gives birth to greater wisdom.

As stated earlier, insight can indeed change who we are, and as a result, change our lives. Looking within, solving mysteries, and finding answers that long eluded us is very liberating and can even be exhilarating. Most often, we feel relief; however, sometimes we might find ourselves in uncharted territory, and as a result, we may feel a bit uneasy. Sometimes we have become so used to relating to others, ourselves, and the world in a certain way, that when our insight leads us to change, we suddenly find ourselves relating in new ways we are not accustomed to. Often we welcome this because having positive, affirming experiences is better than having negative experiences. However, sometimes we can get used to our negative behaviors or ways of relating. After all, it is what we know.

As we excavate ourselves using the tool of insight, and as we respond in merciful and healing ways, we begin living a new life in which we can relate differently with ourselves and others, change our responses to situations, have better experiences, feel lighter and more joyful, and engage life more fully. It is okay and normal if we feel that it takes some getting used to. It's like when we go into a dark room and turn the lights on, and our eyes hurt temporarily as they adjust to the brightness. We can be quite confident in the fact that, with a little time, we will soon adjust to our new life and begin reaping the benefits.

CHAPTER 3

Time and Age
The Great Revealers of the Soul

O<small>UR LIVES ARE MUCH LIKE</small> a snow globe. We accumulate experiences, and all the potential fruits or ills that come from them are like snowflakes that can become stirred up. As time passes, whatever is unresolved settles to the bottom like debris. But in the aftermath of a painful event, at certain ages or during certain life stages, the snow globe gets disturbed. Suddenly, the debris that had settled on the bottom gets stirred up, and we are forced to face what we assumed was in the past but was, in fact, only lying dormant. Our goal is to navigate our lives in such a way that when the snow globe of our experiences gets shaken, the beautiful flakes of resilience, hope, and peace rise to the top, rather than the unresolved debris.

When we have painful experiences in early life, the years afterward may seem quiet. There may be few signs of distress or struggle. We may even go decades or more thinking we are at peace with events of the past. Perhaps the only evidence that we have had distressing experiences is a subtle lingering sadness, fleeting feelings of loss, and/or chronic low-level anxiety. Many of us may just keep functioning on that level, staying in that seemingly fine state for the rest of our days. However, it is not unusual for more troublesome signs of unresolved experiences to surface many years after the stressors have ceased.

Our painful experiences can stay dormant in us for many years because the unconscious mind has a way of knowing when we are ready to deal with something. However, when a certain trigger resonates with us, especially if we have reached a place or stage in life when we have the time and energy to deal with it, previously unfelt pain can surface with intensity.

As our lives progress, we will all arrive at life-stage transitions. Naturally, we will have to make normal adjustments, and negative feelings about life changes will exist to some extent. There is no panacea or formula that can prevent us from having normal feelings about changes that occur in our lives, and these changes often trigger an incongruence between our cognitions and emotions. *I know I'm here temporarily,* we might think to ourselves. *I shouldn't get too attached to my life in this world. So why am I keeping an emotional grip on this world and feeling threatened by the passage of time and by life-stage transitions?* For many of us, our struggle might be due to a fear of death, and we realize we have some faith work to do. But sometimes we sense that we are struggling too much. We tell ourselves, and others tell us too, that our feelings are normal; however, in our "gut" we know we are suffering more than we should as we try to accept a new change or transition.

When our struggle with these transitions feels excessive and disproportionate, this can indicate that something in the present is triggering us, reminding us of unresolved pain from past experiences. This is a sign of transference: the distress of the past and the present get confused. It is like two strands of yarn tangled up in one ball, and to fix the problem, we must set about untangling that ball and separating the past from the present. As we will continue to see in this book, the work each person must do to accomplish this varies.

The goal is not to take away all feelings about the passing of time, aging, and life transitions, but rather to ensure we don't suffer more than we must. We can give ourselves the opportunity to perceive the present through the lens of the present, not the past. But trying to differentiate between what is normal and what is not, between the past and present, can be a very confusing experience. We might try talking to others about their own experiences navigating life stages, in an attempt to gauge whether ours are normal. However, this is increasingly unhelpful, as our society is not good at dealing with grief and loss. In fact, it is widely acknowledged that we tend to distract ourselves through avoidance and self-medicating, by consuming anything that alleviates emotional pain. Indeed, one of the reasons for our own unresolved pain from the past may be chronic avoidance, which leads to an accumulation of unresolved experiences.

Another reason we have trouble deciding whether our response to a life stage is normal is because there is a wide spectrum of normal responses. Some people might feel the grief more intensely, while others are less sensitive to it. Some mark the passage of time deeply and profoundly, while others are hardly aware of it or of life stages and how they affect us. It is not for us to say which of these responses is right or wrong.

So how, then, can we determine what a normal response to life-stage transitions looks like and whether we are struggling more than the usual amount? And how can we learn to differentiate between the past and present? We need to begin by understanding at what times of life we tend to be most vulnerable to triggers that can bring up our past unresolved experiences.

Time and Age Triggers

Sometimes age—the passing of time, alone—acts as a trigger. There are the infamous zeros and nines, indicating the beginning and end of a decade. There are the ages of our children, if we have them, and the times they reach a certain age and we suddenly find ourselves seized with a persistent melancholy. There is the inevitable onset of gray hairs and wrinkles. At other times, an event signifying a major life-stage change is the trigger—events such as starting college, having children, the empty nest, and retirement. A good example of this is when our child first goes to all-day kindergarten. Suddenly, they are not at the lunch table with us, and the house is quiet at that time of day for the first time since they entered our lives. There are also the last days of elementary school, middle school, and the start of high school. Each one of these milestones is a powerful reminder of the passage of time and that these times we have so enjoyed are temporary and will change. It is okay to mark these milestones with some grief. This is normal and not necessarily indicative of an unresolved past. All too often, we shame ourselves for grieving the small passages in life, thinking that we are somehow ungrateful or that something is wrong with us. The presence of grief does not mean there is an absence of joy or gratitude. All three can coexist.

Normal feelings of grief occur throughout all major life stages, even during childhood. For example, it is not unusual for children to struggle when turning ten. They often feel keenly aware of this milestone because it involves moving from single to double digits. On some level, they begin to sense their childhood is temporary and that they are in the later stages of it. Even at that young age, they become aware that the carefree childhood days will soon pass, that adolescence is approaching and then adulthood.

Sometimes we feel grief not because of the life stage itself but because we enter it and realize a certain milestone or event did not occur. This grief is normal to feel as well. We turn thirty or forty years old and have not yet gotten married or had a relationship, for example, or we reach the end of our childbearing years without having had the opportunity to give birth. There is also the infamous midlife crisis, which can occur any time between ages thirty-five and fifty-five. During such a struggle, we might suddenly find ourselves questioning our life and what we have done, taking stock, and feeling profoundly aware of what we have not yet accomplished. When we reach the last gasps of youth and sense the onset of later adulthood, it can create a sense of urgency to resolve anything unfinished or unresolved. Indeed, resolving the unresolved is an investment for our later years.

Any of these normal life transitions and their accompanying dilemmas can collide head-on with unresolved pain in our lives and become tangled together, exacerbating a sense of crisis. For example, although later life stages can satisfy needs that went unmet during childhood—through having a family, children, or a career, for example—as we exit those stages, we can feel like our lives are losing their underpinning and we are free-falling. A particular life stage may merely serve as a Band-Aid, providing temporary relief to the pain of an unmet childhood need.

Another way this often plays out is that we may have been living vicariously through our children. As our children grow and have the life experiences we did not have, and as we as parents experience a home environment we did not have growing up, our family life can inadvertently become about us rather than mainly them. Then, due to life-stage transitions, our family goes through periods of change such as the conclusion of the grade-school years, children leaving for college, or the empty nest time of life, and we suddenly feel like the past has reappeared in the present and that we are re-experiencing old losses. We may have two layers of grief to navigate when these stages occur. For example, we would have to navigate the conclusion of school-related rituals and traditions not only for our children, but also for us, as we had been enjoying them not only as a parent but through the eyes of the child-part of ourselves that has lingered.

We will observe in these instances that the grief and sense of loss are disproportionate. Suddenly, when change arrives and we must move to the next life stage, our wound is exposed and it hurts as though it has just occurred. We might find ourselves scrambling to heal and get relief before the next life stage is fully upon us. In this instance, we experience not only the normal feelings from the present changes but also our own unresolved grief from past unmet needs. Indeed, time can be a great taskmaster, prompting us to resolve the unresolved.

When Change Reveals the Unresolved

We do indeed respond to change differently, and this could be the source of our discomfort with life-stage transitions. Some of us embrace change and even need it every so often. However, some of us dread it and much prefer that our lives change minimally. But when change feels traumatic or when it causes impairment in our lives, there is a good chance the change is acting as a trigger and bringing up unresolved pain from past experiences. When the arrival of a life stage unmasks something unresolved from our past and causes significant impairment in our lives, we might say to ourselves, "I don't know what happened. I was fine until I reached this age or milestone, and suddenly I began to struggle." Sometimes even just the anticipation of a looming life stage can trigger the unresolved to surface—we might suffer for years as one looms closer, never knowing why. One sign that grief around a life-stage transition has exceeded what is normal and contains unresolved past pain is when the anticipation of a life stage pulls us out of the present moment. We may find we can't really enjoy anything in the present because of the constant shadow of future change. Another sign is when the end or beginning of a life stage feels like a trauma, like the past is happening all over again. No matter how much we tell ourselves the right things, revise and reframe our perceptions, try to laugh at ourselves, or normalize our experience, we can't shake our dread over an impending life change. Something from our past seems to color our perception of the future or present, or our emotions seem to be coming from another time and place.

Each life-stage transition involves change but triggers different fears. For example, change we have no perceived control over contains an element of powerlessness. For those of us with significant, unresolved painful experiences, a life-stage transition can feel like a terrible loss of control. Once again, we feel immobilized. We fear being rendered powerless again, so we avoid the feeling at all costs. Even the normal feeling of powerlessness that comes with a life-stage transition can make us feel anxious or depressed when we feel as if the past is happening all over again, because the presence of powerlessness in traumatic experiences can cause us to have only negative associations with it. This can lead to an excessive need for control in many different, or all, areas of our lives. We can unconsciously develop the mission of being in absolute control over everyone and everything. We do this in an attempt to stop the past from happening again. However, when the great taskmaster of time appears at our backs, pushing us into a new life stage, we can feel blindsided, and it is as though time becomes the abuser. We can feel weak all over again and as a result even experience shame over our perceived weakness or loss of control in the face of time. This is an example of what it could look like to suffer more than we need to during a life-stage transition.

Some life-stage transitions also activate core fears. For example, the transition from adolescence to young adulthood could trigger a fear of failure, which may have been formed by an experience of verbal abuse. In this life stage, we have to deal with adults and authority figures, and this can heighten the fear of past verbal abuse occurring again. The entrance into the workplace, especially, can create a minefield of triggers due to performance pressures, evaluations, and the many interpersonal interactions. Suddenly, we feel like we are re-experiencing past situations that subjected us to harsh criticism or rejection. We also feel heightened pressure to get married and to minimize the time of singleness. As peers get married, the pressure begins to rapidly increase on those who are still single. This can activate feelings or fears of failure from a past experience. Though there is still great youth at the young-adult life stage, the transition can still be challenging.

There are some other major ways that life-stage transitions can trigger feelings or fears of loss that are disproportionate. For example, if we grew up in a home with out-of-control behavior and unpredictability, we may have an aversion to change later in life. This alone can make life stages more difficult than they need to be. Or, we may have experienced more change in our first eighteen years of life than many do a in a lifetime. This can make us feel burned out and tired of change. Unknowingly, we can find ourselves settling in and getting comfortable, even too comfortable, in a particular life stage. We can go so far as to somehow trick ourselves, even on an unconscious level, into the mindset that this stage of life will last forever.

When We Can't Let Go of What We Didn't Have as Children

We may especially find ourselves getting too comfortable in a life stage where we have been able to build a life that is everything we didn't have when we were growing up. We can build a life marked with peace, consistency, safety, and predictability. We can have a home where, instead of strife or conflict, there is love. A home where our children are carefree and nurtured. Having these experiences in the present, though they contrast with our past, is therapeutic and a kind of massage for our soul. We may even relish the opportunity to do things our way now, rather than settling for the unpredictable and negative behavior we were accustomed to in our childhood homes. Doing things our way gives us an opportunity to fulfill a pledge many of us made in our younger years, that when we have our own family, we will never do what was done to us and will not allow our children to experience what we did. As noble a goal as this is, we can inadvertently forget that our present life stage is temporary, and that change is an inevitable part of life. We subtly slip into the assumption that somehow our current circumstances will last forever. Pain from the past can make us hold onto the present too tightly, especially if it embodies everything our life growing up was not. Then, when time passes and change occurs, we feel the changes should not happen. It becomes hard to normalize the life-stage changes and we start to feel powerless, as though our past is repeating itself by robbing us again of what we did not have growing up. We suffer the loss we experienced earlier in our lives all over again. This is another example of how we can suffer unnecessarily when an unresolved past makes us feel like present change is traumatic.

During such times, it becomes apparent that our present life is not quite resolving our pain from the past. The arrival or departure of a certain life stage forces us to realize that unconsciously we have been waiting for the family of origin we never had to appear. Without awareness, we can have a deep, unceasing hope that one day our family of origin will have a revelation or epiphany and will suddenly be the family they should have been but were not. It is as though we keep a silent vigil of hope in our hearts. We can carry this deep hope for individuals; however, we can also do this with family systems. At the core of this hope, and indeed what drives it, are unmet needs yearning to be satisfied. When time passes and certain life stages arrive, it becomes increasingly clear that this is not going to happen. Perhaps we realize this through the aging of certain family members, deaths, or by reaching a certain age ourselves. These life events signal to us that our long-hoped-for changes are not going to occur and that the proverbial ship has sailed. This can leave us with a profound sense of grief and loss. Until we work through this and arrive at a place of acceptance, a deep resignation can set in, causing us to shut down and disengage from life.

This type of grief often goes deep. When operating unconsciously, it can, like all forms of grief, make us do peculiar things like seek to meet unmet needs through other people in ways that might not be healthy or fair to them. This might take the form of us feeling drawn to certain individuals because they remind us of someone else in our life. Or we might seek out certain relationships in an attempt to reassemble our family of origin. We may also develop unrealistic expectations of relationships and those around us. While this might seem harmless, it may cause others to feel overwhelmed or unduly pressured. Either way, meeting unmet needs in these ways is not a long-term solution, nor will these behaviors lead to resolution of the unmet needs. What we are trying to do is stitch together the life we never had in an effort to get certain needs met; however, it is not a good long-term fix. When we do this, our life might feel like it is made up of patchwork pieces, never fully repaired, whereas the lives of others seem so whole and intact.

There is nothing wrong with seeking in the present what we did not have growing up—it is the right and healthy thing to do, so that we do not recreate the mistakes of our family of origin. However, true resolution of these unmet needs can only come from our adult self. We do this by identifying, coming to terms with, and answering the questions related to the unmet needs that we asked as children but never were able to answer—often because we lacked the developmental knowledge and skills to do so. These questions linger, and in time eventually resurface and yearn to be answered. Until they are answered and resolved, we run the risk of seeking the answers through others. This tends to set us up for disappointment, as others cannot do what our family of origin was supposed to do. They cannot go back in time and meet those needs at the time we needed them to be met. Our adult self will have to do the work to get those questions answered. Then, when we have met those needs ourselves, our life will no longer feel like patchwork pieces, but rather, whole and seamless.

The unmet needs and corresponding questions stem from disruptions in what children and adults need most: a sense of safety, love, predictability, and confidence that caretakers can usually be trusted to fulfill in their roles. A child needs to know that their mother and father will always be there to meet their needs and to protect them. Breakdowns in these fundamental areas leave a profound mark on the child or adolescent.

Many of us are quick to dismiss certain painful life experiences because we do not believe they were severe or frightening enough to leave that mark. Someone who grew up with an alcoholic parent, for instance, might assume their parent's addiction wasn't an issue because they weren't an "angry drunk"—they never displayed destructive or frightening behavior. However, children have an innate understanding of what a parent should be, of what is right and wrong, and when they perceive a parent doing something wrong, it leaves a mark or injury. A violation or betrayal occurs—suddenly, a child's sense of security is threatened because they no longer perceive their mother or father as safe, predictable, or reliable. The loss of certainty that the parent will be there for them is a real loss. Not only has doubt entered the relationship but also a profound disappointment that often leads to incongruence as the child struggles to reconcile this new way of perceiving their parent with what they knew before.

When our unanswered questions from childhood resurface in adulthood, we can find ourselves feeling profound loss again, and we can begin now to identify what questions we had—and indeed still have—related to our unmet needs. Many such questions are nearly universal: "Why are they doing this?" "Who will take care of me?" "Was I not good enough for them?" "Why did I get parents who behave this way?" Because young minds lack the cognitive tools to answer these questions, they often jump to unhealthy beliefs instead, like deep shame, inadequacy, and loneliness. Inevitably, the child or adolescent will also try to fill the void by attempting to plug the gap in their parents' parenting, which can open the door for over-controlling behaviors. This will be discussed more in the next chapter.

The Christian View of Time and Life Stages

We have so far in this chapter covered how time and age, while presenting normal challenges to all of us, can also be powerful triggers for unresolved pain in our lives and reveal to us where our unfinished work lies. Our goal is to move through these life-stage transitions peacefully, and our Faith, indeed, does give us what we need in order to do so. However, unresolved pain from past experiences can disrupt our ability to utilize what our Faith teaches. "What earthly glory goes unmixed with grief?" the funeral service of the Orthodox Church asks. In other words, all joy and pleasure will pass away, and we will have to let go of it all. The entire funeral service is a sobering reminder of the brevity of our lives.

We must often remind ourselves of our purpose. Our calling is to participate in deification, or theosis: to become through grace what God is by nature. We must seek to abide in communion with God by living how He intended us to live. God calls us to live in such a way that our fallen nature is sanctified through the healing of our wounds, so that we can love and be loved as we were meant to. The time we have been given in this world is for this purpose.

An important part of the process of theosis is to age and navigate life stages with grace and dignity, and to retain mentoring roles for as long as we can. Later life stages are often marked by losses, both real and perceived. However, each stage of our life also offers the opportunity for us to play a new role and find a new purpose. Often, we relinquish mentoring roles too quickly as we age, too quickly indulging the feeling that no one needs us anymore. Despite many affirmations to the contrary from adult children, grandchildren, great-grandchildren, and from any individual in our lives, we check out prematurely and dismiss our worth and purpose. Yet it is a noble goal to hang in as long as we can in a mentoring role and to resist the temptation of feeling betrayed by time and life changes such as our children getting older, retirement, and other losses. During these transitions, we often feel that life is done with us; however, maybe it is we who have decided to be done with life.

When we disengage from life, this is very tragic because we deny our children, grandchildren, friends, and acquaintances a presence of wisdom, support, and comfort. Our disengagement feels like a great loss to the people in our lives. We can easily forget how important it is, especially for younger generations, to know we are there, that we love them, and that we will help in any way should they need it. Indeed, all these things are a profound comfort to the people in our lives. We would do well to deliberately decide what kind of presence we want to be to our children and grandchildren, and all the people we are connected with, as we age. We have far more power and ability to retain purpose and roles in our later years than we realize. There is always power in our perceptions, especially in the later life stages. If, indeed, we perceive later life stages as only times of loss, then we will be more prone to depression and the temptation to check out of our life long before God desires us to do so.

God calls us to a unique balance throughout our life, which is critical for navigating all life stages, not only the later stages. The balance consists of the effort to retain our purpose in this world while also waiting for the Kingdom of God. We engage each present moment and the life God has given us, but at the same time, we keep unceasing vigil in our hearts for the main story of our life: the return home to be as we were meant to be from the beginning. The monastics of the Church provide a perfect model of this. They faithfully tend to their earthly tasks and responsibilities yet keep perpetual watch in their hearts. Monastics display little to no struggle in navigating life stages because for them, the role and purpose of seeking communion with God through ascetical striving lasts as long as they have their breath. Also, the end of one traditional life stage and the beginning of another pass by rather unnoticed by a monastic, as they do not define their existence by earthly obligations tied to a particular age. They have achieved an emotional and spiritual immunity to the passage of time. Instead of holding on too tightly and investing in this world, they travel lightly, remaining faithful to the present moment and those around them, all the while keeping their internal gaze focused on the Kingdom of God. Although we do not live in a monastery, we can practice this same balance in our own life.

In reality, without life stages we would never want to leave this world—we would never want to let go. We can see God's wisdom in this. The progression of age and the letting go of life stages weans us from our earthly life. Each life-stage transition gives us the opportunity to let go of a part of our existence in this world, even if, at times, our faith seems weak and we feel immobilized in the face of change as a life stage approaches. Indeed, one could argue that this letting go is ascetical—if we navigate life stages peacefully and with acceptance, rather than with resistance and avoidance, we practice self-denial to obtain the Kingdom of God. We trust God's plan for us, which is not to remain in this fallen world forever. Our life is like a story, and life stages are the chapters. God holds us in His lap, like a parent does a child, and is present as the story progresses. Eventually a chapter concludes and the page must be turned to a new chapter. However, sometimes we resist the turning of the page. We become the child who grabs hold of the corner of the page so it can't be turned. As we would with our own children, God gently engages us and encourages us to turn the page. In essence, He urges us to trust Him and to follow the story. It is indeed a leap of faith and a letting go, and just as God *gently* waits for us to be ready to move on to the next chapter, so we must be gentle and merciful with ourselves.

Our unresolved wounds yearn to be healed before we depart this world. However, the longer they remain unresolved, the more they can cause us to resist life-stage transitions and disrupt healthy participation in God's plan for us. When this happens, our struggle with the life-stage transition often causes us to believe we are having a faith crisis or that our faith is weak. But it is not a sin to struggle. It is not a sin to have feelings about life changes. It is not a sin to grieve or feel pain. We just need to keep moving and work through it so we do not stay stuck in that space. While sometimes we do just need to fall back on our faith and refocus, other times we struggle in a way that is disproportionate to reality, indicating there is something hindering our capacity to use our faith and live according to our Christian worldview. In this case, it is possible that certain memories have not been stored away properly, a topic that will be covered more in Chapter 6.

CHAPTER 4

Seeing Our Struggles in the Larger Picture
Identifying Roles, Life Projections,
and Abandonment

T RYING TO LIVE OUR PRESENT life story while the unresolved past disrupts us is like trying to listen to two songs at once. We put on one song to listen to, but there's another song playing in the background and our attention becomes divided between the two. We don't know which one to focus on. At times, we might switch our attention back and forth from one song to the other involuntarily. Each time we do, our behavior changes, depending on the mood of the song we are listening to more closely. In a similar way, sometimes the song of our past can become dominant, and we start "listening" to it rather than the song of the present. This can confuse us and those around us. However, once we resolve the unintended song of the past, we can give our full attention and devotion to the present.

As just covered in the previous chapter, while time's passing or life-stage transitions can be triggering, sometimes our challenges stem from the past rather than the present or future. We may attempt to prevent something unresolved in the past from happening again by engaging in difficult behaviors or getting entangled in negative perceptions. One way this happens, and the focus of this chapter, is when we get stuck in a learned role that is no longer functional. The mind is amazing—we can live years, decades, or even an entire lifetime acting out the patterns of an old story without ever realizing it, even though we may struggle because of this.

It is difficult to become aware of this, as we tend to focus on what is closest to us—namely, feelings, and what is happening in our present life. When trying to alleviate our pain, we are tempted to fixate on the symptoms of our struggles rather than the source. Our vision tends to be myopic. We fix our gaze on individual trees while missing the larger forest of our struggle. It's much like trying to figure out the storyline of a novel while only reading random sentences out of order. Certainly, writing our life story or narrative can help with this (see Chapter 1) because it familiarizes us with the story of our struggles and puts them in a context. However, we also need to know what to look for when we step back and examine our behavior patterns, troublesome emotions, and inner conflicts. If we lack awareness of how a painful experience, wound, or a role from the past is affecting us, we can spend our whole life unconsciously repeating it or acting out the same role. These patterns can become the driving force in our life. They can be disruptive and even work against fundamental aspects of our faith practices. Yet most of us can't help but focus only on what we see—the symptoms and pain these patterns cause—because their sources lie so deep.

When we step back and take a larger view of our life and the context in which the struggles and symptoms occur, we can learn to understand the functions and purposes they serve. Oftentimes, as soon as we realize this, we can recognize them as dysfunctional, unhelpful, and obsolete, and we can see that they need to stop. We realize we have been following the wrong narrative, that is, the narrative of the past. This is half the battle. The other half is healing from the original experience that caused the struggles and learning to not react to the triggers.

Once we see our struggles as deeper than just the symptoms we are having, we will need to determine what roles we have learned to play because of certain experiences from our past. We can live for most of or an entire lifetime never becoming aware of these roles that have played such a powerful part in driving our behaviors and emotions. We often learn these roles when we are young, and they tend to be unhealthy, unrealistic, and the cause of much of our grief. They usually result from the failure of early key figures in our lives to fulfill basic elements of their roles in relation to us. We should never have had to play these roles. They often lead us to create impossible life missions that at best result in us putting too much pressure on ourselves, or at worst drive us to over-function and cause distress both to ourselves and others. They can also cause severe disruption to our spiritual lives.

While we may experience dramatic relief and peace just from identifying and acknowledging a certain role we have been playing, coming to terms with and healing from it is a longer process. We may have to work through how we feel about having had to play such an unfair role for so long. Usually we feel grief, not to mention a profound sense of letting go of the role, as we recognize how dysfunctional and unrealistic the role was.

In addition to feeling grief, we may also feel adrift. As distressing as our unhealthy role(s) may have been, it was all we knew. When we try to let it go, we suddenly find ourselves in unfamiliar territory—it's a profound life change. We have to take our time and fully come to terms with the past, let it go, grieve the loss of the purpose or role (however dysfunctional it was), and replace it with a healthy one. If we don't go through this process, we risk creating a void that leaves us feeling depressed or adrift, as though we are spiritually or emotionally unemployed. A deep and existential sense of "now what?" fills us. If that is not our role, then who are we? Often adding to the aggravation is the reality that we adopted these roles because an early or critical caregiver was unable to play *their* role—namely, to provide us with protection, stability, consistency, love, safety, and predictability. We may not have had a parental role model to help us learn the healthy roles we should play. As a result, we were left to fill the void left by the parent.

The Parentified Child

A parentified child is someone who was forced to assume adult responsibilities far sooner than they should have. While the term may seem noble to those unfamiliar with it, it is actually tragic. The child pays a steep cost for assuming adult responsibilities before they have the cognitive tools to shoulder such a burden. When children assume adult roles and responsibilities in a family, the burden becomes a long-term source of grief and stress in their lives.

Common Issues That Can Lead to Parentification of Children in a Family

» **The death of a parent,** especially in cases when the surviving parent puts too much pressure or responsibility on the child to fill the role of the deceased parent.

» **Divorce,** especially if parents look to their kids to play the caretaker role, whether emotionally or by asking them to shoulder household responsibilities previously delegated to the parent who left the home. Also, sometimes one parent may use the child as a confidant.

» **Addiction.** If a parent has an addiction to drugs or alcohol, likely they will cease acting like a parent at times. When this occurs, no one is in control in the home. This frightens children and can be traumatic for them. They then try to fill the power vacuum.

» **Mental illness.** If the suffering is unmanaged, there might be times when the parent or parents are unavailable or unable to fulfill basic household responsibilities.

» **Unresolved pain and woundedness** in the parents themselves. In this case, the parents have times when they simply cannot parent because of their own emotional baggage, which can result in their child shouldering burdens, cares, and responsibilities that are not theirs to carry.

It is important to note that some causes of parentification are more subtle and are not included above. We might not have experienced any situations as dramatic as those listed; however, sometimes we were burdened just a bit too much by things that could have caused us to assume more responsibility than warranted for a child.

The Two Types of Parentification:
Instrumental and Emotional

Instrumental parentification occurs when a child experiences parentification for logistical purposes, for example, when they must help maintain the household and do adult chores and tasks. They may have been expected to cook and clean more than is appropriate for a child, or to parent younger siblings by putting them to bed and getting them ready for school. They may even have had to drive illegally to pick up a drunk parent, or make sure bills were paid.

Emotional parentification, on the other hand, happens when the child assumes responsibilities for the emotional well-being of the family. One or both parents may look to the child to support them emotionally. As a result, the child hears things they should not, and they have to carry heavy burdens. Finally, they end up parenting their parents. The situation becomes a role reversal. Also, when they assume emotional responsibility for the family, they can learn to believe it is their job to control the behaviors in the home and to make sure no one gets upset. For example, when the parents fight or have conflict, at times no one may be parenting. This forces the children, or one child, to step in and try to control the situation. This is devastating. The child then must grow up with the added responsibility of managing the behavior of the parents. In doing so, they also try to learn to manage their parents' moods and emotions. They quickly and unconsciously learn that if they can just keep everyone happy in the home, there will be no conflict. It's clear that playing such roles early in life can burden children with undue stress and cause them grief long into their adult life because they end up assuming responsibility for other people's emotions.

71

The Painful Legacy of Parentification

As children develop, it is critical that they not become psychologically overwhelmed at any point. If they do, an emotional injury takes place that may lie dormant for years but will eventually yearn for resolution and healing later in life. Our minds know when something happened that should not have happened, when some aspect of ourselves has been violated or betrayed. To cope in the moment and respond to the crisis at hand, we tend to suppress and bury away this awareness. Eventually, however, we will have to come to terms with the parentification, either because over-functioning causes us problems as adults or a life stage triggers our minds to yearn for resolution and healing.

When a parentified child assumes adult responsibilities, they are forced to try and manage the unmanageable and control the uncontrollable. For this reason, control remains a central need as they become adults—as parentified children, we learned that if we did not over-function, our family system would collapse or even cease to exist. We can see the enormous pressure placed on parentified children. A child simply cannot take on the role and responsibilities of an adult—it's mission impossible for the child. While they may manage to keep up the role for a time, eventually—in childhood or adulthood—it will unravel.

Sadly, even if the problematic situation resolves itself or the child grows up and leaves the home environment, the damage has already been done. Learned parentification does not just go away but follows the child into adulthood. It is well established that parentified children are more likely to become adults who struggle with anxiety and depression because of the pressure they put on themselves and the unreasonable expectations they have for themselves. Parentified children often grow up feeling that no matter how well they do, their efforts are never good enough. This is because they were put in a situation where they could not fix the family deficits or the failure of their parents to parent properly.

Parentified children-turned-adults also tend to suffer from shame and guilt because no matter how hard they try to hold the family together and compensate for the parents' weaknesses, their work is not really ever enough. Inevitably, the problems of the parents will overwhelm the family system, and in the end, the parentified child cannot fix or change the dysfunctional parents' behavior. A parentified child will carry the heavy burden of self-blame because they believe things turned out as they did because they were not good enough. They failed. Tragically, parents may have even communicated this to their children, in an attempt to shift blame and responsibility. No matter how successful and high functioning a once-parentified adult becomes, deep down inside they retain a gnawing feeling of inadequacy. Worse yet, because they learned early that their job is to manage the unmanageable and control the uncontrollable, they set themselves up for perceived failure as they over-function in their adult life and feel that the responsibility is all on them to stop bad things from happening. Then, when the inevitable happens and they cannot control the uncontrollable, they become saddled with deep feelings of failure, shame, and guilt. Eventually, they may reach a point in their life where they become tired from this mission impossible. Resentment and bitterness will set in once they realize the role was unfair.

Parentified children also suffer fundamental losses. On a deep, sometimes even buried, level, the parentified child is aware that something occurred that should not have. They missed out on the carefree and predictable life children need in order to develop in a healthy way. They also don't remember really being a child, and they have a shortage or absence of lighthearted memories from childhood. Additionally, they experienced the loss of their parents because parentification indicates something missing in the parents' presence and care. The child lost their parents precisely when they needed them most. Add to this another layer of injury because the very people who were supposed to protect them were the ones causing distress and even trauma. The profound loss of protection needs to be grieved later in adult life. It can also lead to a chronic, deep, and profound sense of disappointment we carry the rest of our lives until we can recognize and resolve it.

Until then, that profound and deep disappointment may manifest itself as a lack of tolerance for what we perceive as disappointing behavior in others. When others fail to meet our expectations, their behavior acts as a trigger. Although it's tempting to dismiss this or assume we are being too sensitive, it's more than that. The disappointing behavior activates all the pain and hurt from the core disappointment in our family of origin, so our responses to this trigger can cause us to act in ways that are disproportionate to the situation. We might suddenly pull back and create distance between us and the one who disappointed us, for example. We might sense that we perceive others in black-or-white terms, as all good or all bad (or disappointing). Or we may thrive in relationships until the other person does something so disagreeable that we feel betrayed on some level. Deep down, we understand that we weren't, but emotionally we feel sad, hurt, or even angry. We might engage in a reenactment by retaliating and making others feel how we feel. For example, if someone does not acknowledge us in a way we expected or hoped for, the encounter may trigger feelings of inadequacy. We then ignore them or give them the cold shoulder so that they might feel like we do. We may not realize or understand that the deep wound of our parents not protecting us when we needed them the most is indeed our core unresolved experience of disappointment. And because we have not dealt with it, the pain of it leaks out every time someone in the present does something disappointing. This can make it hard for us to maintain close relationships, as we constantly feel disappointed by people and find ourselves on an unending quest to discover that one person who does not disappoint.

We may have learned several types of roles if we were emotionally parentified. They tend to be chronic and long-standing defense mechanisms that we acquired to cope when we were robbed of the control and predictability any child needs and should have. In the following section we will discuss the roles of protector and people-pleaser.

The Role of Protector

It is a normal, even positive, quality to be willing to protect others. However, acting as the protector is only healthy when a clear and real threat exists. In such situations, attempting to exert control over a situation is appropriate and helpful. In fact, we might be considered cowardly, selfish, or irresponsible if we did not try to keep others safe from danger. Sometimes, however, we learn to play a protector role because of painful early life experiences, especially those where we did not receive the protection we should have. When protective behavior is born from unresolved pain, it can become unhealthy and disruptive to us and others. In our attempts to stop the past from ever happening again, we tend to exhibit this kind of demeanor when it is not necessary—namely, when there is no actual danger or threat, just a perceived one. On the surface this might seem noble and chivalrous, but in these instances, the protector is trying to manage situations and events that don't need to be controlled and are not threats. This can be very frustrating to those who live with the protector, and they may eventually feel smothered, restricted, or controlled.

Typically, we deem something a threat if it shares some common trait of our unresolved experience. As mentioned earlier, a common trait of situations we see as threatening is powerlessness. We might become anxious and over-function if someone close to us endures something we think will make them powerless. Perhaps they have to get surgery, go camping, take a trip, or leave for college. It might also happen when our loved one finds him or herself in a situation where others make decisions that will affect them—for example, grades at school, a job application, or a college application. The protector might feel far more anxious than their loved one, who is the one going through those experiences, which are quite normal, because witnessing their loved one experience perceived powerlessness is intolerable. The protector just cannot risk that their loved one might experience emotional suffering in the form of disappointment, rejection, grief, or loss. In the end, they project their life experience onto those they love, and the loved one on some level feels this projection being imposed on them. As a result, they may attempt to assert their independence more than they need to and even manifest passive-aggressive behavior in order to secure some sense of autonomy. At best, this can leave the one playing the protector role feeling hurt, rejected, and unappreciated; at worst, they might feel re-traumatized.

Ultimately, the protector is setting themselves up for perceived failure. This is because an unrealistic need for control lies at the core of their past-driven behavior. The protector inevitably ends up trying to control the universe to keep their loved ones and themselves safe. Sooner or later, these attempts to control the uncontrollable will not succeed, leaving the protector feeling like a failure—weak, powerless, and ashamed, and believing that despite their best efforts, the past is happening all over again. No matter how skillfully and adeptly the protector influences situations so they will be favorable for their loved ones, sooner or later they will encounter forces they cannot control, like the progression of time and aging. Eventually, those we love grow older and move on to the next life stage. Children go to college and parents experience decreasing physical abilities due to age or sickness. The person in protector mode will have to go through the painful process of coming to terms with this. More about this process will be explained later in this chapter.

When the protector realizes that control, and thus perceived protection, is unattainable, it is very difficult for them to conceive of the possibility that everything will still be okay. They have become so accustomed to associating powerlessness with imminent disaster that the idea of good things happening in the presence of powerlessness is hard to work through. This often leaves the protector feeling that they have suffered profound failure and defeat and thus will be left to spend the rest of their days watching life events play out without any control. A deep sense of resignation can set in, and without intervention, they can fall into depression, feeling checked out and disengaged.

The Role of the People-Pleaser

Another role we might find ourselves playing is that of people-pleaser. For some adults who had to take on adult burdens as children, the most frightening moments occurred when their parents or caregivers became upset. It doesn't take a child very long to reason that if they can prevent Mom or Dad from getting upset, then everything will be okay. The child, rather than accepting their own powerlessness and lack of safety (which, depending on their age, they lack the cognitive skills to do), will assume responsibility for the emotional state of their caregivers. This allows them to feel some sense of control, however unhealthy and unrealistic.

Though this is a coping mechanism—an attempt to make sense of a frightening situation—it unfortunately stays active long after the stressful situation has ended. The people-pleasing tendency to assume responsibility for others' moods and behaviors stays intact and follows the parentified child throughout their life. Most of us can readily acknowledge that it is not our fault if someone else is upset. We might even be able to concede that even if someone is upset directly with us, that does not necessarily mean we are to blame. Perhaps we have mastered the ability, when appropriate and accurate, to say and believe, "This is their problem, not mine, and therefore it is not my job to fix it." However, for those of us who were parentified children and are now adults, it is not so simple. Even if we can tell ourselves all these things in a cognitive sense, we still feel emotionally that we are somehow at fault if someone becomes angry or upset. We can't shake the sense that despite our best efforts, talents, and hard work, this still happens with people in our environment, which can leave us with a deep sense of failure and shame, as though their feelings are our failure. We don't know why we feel this way because we don't realize we have been living our whole life with a false belief: as long as everyone is happy, we are safe, but if someone gets upset, that means we are unsafe.

When they were growing up, the parentified child was not safe when someone became upset—Mom or Dad's anger was an existential threat to the entire family. These children then become adults who cannot understand why they feel like the world is ending if someone close to them gets upset or angry. We can see here how learned childhood beliefs can linger into adulthood until they are discovered, revised, and unlearned. Until these beliefs are addressed, they can be devastating and debilitating.

Life Projections

Part of the ability to make sense of our struggles and see them in a bigger context is learning to identify life projections. A life projection is a type of transference, which is when something unresolved from the past becomes triggered and active in the present. However, rather than being situational or fleeting, a life projection involves chronically and perpetually living according to a past story rather than our present life story. (To get a sense of what this looks like in real life, see the Case Study section below).

Life projections are powerful and largely unconscious. When

we engage in this form of transference, we go through life never really understanding why we tend to over-function, have chronic issues with control, and disproportionately struggle so much in certain situations or during certain life changes. This is because some aspect of our past has been superimposed on the present. The people and experiences that shaped our early life story may be long gone, but deep inside we feel as if they are still present with us. Life projections can even occur when we are aware of our past and have good insight into what we went through growing up. They are very hard to detect until we become aware of this phenomenon or someone else points it out to us.

Many of us know our life story. But have we asked ourselves whether the past is still playing out in our life? In other words, how much of our struggle comes from an unconscious mission to prevent the past from happening again? Sometimes we are convinced on a deep emotional level that as we approach certain ages or life stages, the past will recur. We typically are not conscious of this fear, but we feel it nonetheless. It can be a very confusing experience.

Mark: A Case Study in Recognizing Life Projections

Mark is a married forty-four-year-old male with three children aged twelve, fourteen, and sixteen. When his eldest two children turned nine and seven, he began to experience periods of sadness that caused him to ruminate on how quickly his children were growing up. He felt an intense sense of loss, especially on their birthdays, but could not figure out why. His oldest child's last day of elementary school was particularly difficult for him.

As Mark realized how sensitive he was to things coming to an end, he began to wonder whether this was a learned pattern—the result of some past life experience—or just his temperament. "Why am I assigning a meaning of loss to normal life milestones?" he would ask himself. When he tried to see if friends and others around him wrestled with similar feelings, they only reported fleeting moments of sadness over their children growing up. But this, they said, was accompanied by positive feelings and perceptions—they felt excited for their children and enjoyed each age and stage of their lives.

As Mark's children continued to grow up, he found it increasingly challenging to be joyful and stay in the present moment with them. His mind frequently wandered to the future, to the time when his children would no longer be children but adolescents, ready to leave for college. This struggle escalated significantly when his oldest child entered their first year of high school, and he felt plagued with an overwhelming feeling of powerlessness. As his eldest progressed through high school, Mark continued to feel that their looming graduation amounted to an existential threat to the family. His struggles were coming to a head, as though ready to splinter. When Mark tried to imagine life after the last of his children left for college, he couldn't perceive or envision anything. He saw only a massive void, as though the family would cease to exist altogether.

He wrestled with these fears and perceptions, which on a cognitive level he could recognize as distorted. Time and again, he reminded himself that it was normal—a sign of a healthy life—for children to grow up and become adults. They couldn't stay children forever. He tried practicing gratitude—it would work for a moment, but soon he would be back to dreading the future. He began to become aware of a deep belief repeating itself in his head: "I cannot stop this."

The more aware Mark became of the unshakeable perceptions that were operating within him, the more he realized that, on some level, he was expecting himself to be able to stop time, to stop his children from growing up and leaving the house. Mark began counseling to resolve his struggles, and it started becoming clear that sometimes the words "I can't stop it" also carried a past-tense meaning: "I *couldn't* stop it." This, he knew, was a clue. The past-tense form of the belief was related to his childhood years. Mark's parents had fought terribly throughout his childhood, eventually divorcing when he was a teenager. On some level, he now realized, he had been holding on to the belief that he should have been able to stop the family from falling apart.

Finally, during a session with his counselor, the counselor asked Mark about his relationship with his wife. They had a great relationship, Mark said. They enjoyed being together.

"How did things go for your parents after you and your siblings left the house?" the counselor then asked.

Mark explained that as soon as he—the youngest child—left home, his parents separated and divorced.

"Do you see what's going on here?" the counselor asked. "Mark, you're not your parents."

For the first time, Mark could see the massive life projection he had been engaging in for the previous seven years. It was precisely after he had begun college that his parents had divorced, and the family as he knew it had come to end. Mark had been unconsciously projecting the trajectory of his family of origin onto his present family, with the deep sense that somehow what had happened to his childhood family would happen again. He believed the catalyst for his family coming to an end—a child leaving for college—would be the same for his present family.

This discovery led to many other realizations for Mark. He now understood why he had felt so threatened by the passage of time—he had been living with the belief that his family had an expiration date, and with the sense that upon entering a certain life stage, the family would cease to exist. After all, that is what had happened to his family of origin. When his parents divorced, Mark experienced it as the death of his family. This is why he had been suffering so badly.

The moment all of this became clear to Mark, the past and the present separated. He felt immediate relief. Suddenly he could imagine his future for the first time. He could see a life for himself and his wife even after his children left for college. He also could finally believe and feel that the family would not die or cease to exist even when the last child left home. The family system would endure.

Mark began to understand why this life projection had occurred. He had never healed from his parents' divorce and how it had so profoundly affected his family. He had never fully grieved the death of his family, which had never recovered from the divorce. As Mark saw it, a profound shadow of loss had hung over the family ever since the divorce twenty years ago. He and his parents and siblings never again gathered at a dinner table or even under the same roof. It was as though each family member lived alone on their own deserted island in the wake of this great loss. Mark also understood some of his behaviors better now, like why he always liked to drive past the homes his family had lived in when was growing up. In retrospect, it was like he was driving past old ruins of a now-extinct civilization.

We can see how profoundly Mark's mind marked the trauma and loss of his parents' divorce and the subsequent breakup of the family, and how, once he separated the past and the present and went through the healing work he had not been able to do at the time, he gained a sense of mastery over his own life story. For the first time, Mark felt excitement for the future. This made him a better father, as could now talk to his kids about college and lean into what he had previously avoided.

Abandonment: The Great Underminer of Stability

When we consider the word *abandonment*, we tend to think of more dramatic forms of it—a parent walking out on their child or dropping them off somewhere, never to see or be seen by them again. As a result, many of us are quick to assume we have never experienced abandonment. However, the pain and trauma of abandonment take many forms, many of them subtler than the above examples. Fear of abandonment is normal—no one wants to be abandoned. No matter how healthy and normal our upbringing might have been, we will still find abandonment unpleasant. As human beings we are meant for social connection. However, what if we have endured experiences involving a failed relationship with a caretaker and protector? In this section, we will explore how our ability to relate with others can become so disrupted that social connection itself becomes an emotional minefield.

Part of healing is finding the right words to express the core aspect of our experience. We often know something is wrong but cannot quite state what it is because the fear of abandonment can be subtle and hard to detect. Additionally, we may simply minimize our struggles by believing that we are just insecure, too sensitive, and/or have low self-esteem, and if we recognize abandonment only in its more dramatic manifestations, we may never consider it as part of our life story. When caregivers are unable to be there for us emotionally by protecting, providing for, and comforting us during times of need, this also constitutes abandonment. The developing child's mind is highly sensitive. The early bonds we form with our parents, and our confidence in those bonds, is critical for stable relationships throughout life. In homes governed by chronic conflict, addiction, mental illness, or just parents who have not done their own healing work, there is a significant chance that the children will experience inconsistency and unpredictability. When a baby cries, they seek comfort. When a child hurts themselves, they seek help. When a child is afraid, they seek reassurance. In the face of danger, a child needs to know someone will protect them. When these basic needs are not met—when a basic sense of trust and security is not achieved in the parent-child relationship—attachment issues can occur. In essence, the baby or child never learns to trust that they will be cared for, responded to, and affirmed. This can have debilitating effects into adulthood. It is accurate to say that adults do not get abandoned; children get abandoned. As adults we may have experiences that make us *feel* abandoned; however, so long as we do not abandon ourselves and we lean on our faith, we cannot actually be abandoned. This is because we are adults who have the ability to take care of ourselves.

However, for the child it is different because they cannot yet be independent. The child believes, "If you leave me, I will die." When we have experienced a form of abandonment in early life, we tend to become adults who struggle with a fear of abandonment, gnawing insecurity, and anxiety in relationships. We tend to be needy, have trust issues, and have difficulty tolerating ambiguity in relationships.

Abandonment and Relationship Instability

Fear of abandonment can lead to hypervigilance for any sign that we might be rejected or re-experience the type of abandonment we had experienced at an earlier time. This can make it very difficult to tolerate the natural ebbs and flows and normal disagreements that arise from time to time in a relationship. Sometimes someone cannot respond right away to a text message or a phone call. Sometimes they might not always be able to call us as much as we call them. These occurrences are normal in relationships and certainly not indicative that the relationship is bad. However, when we have had unresolved abandonment in our lives, we have a hard time tolerating these natural ambiguities in relationships. We tend to immediately assign meaning to these mild imperfections, things like: the relationship is false, not safe, not reciprocated, or rejection is imminent. We might even tend to perceive others as either all good or all bad, and struggle to accept the reality that people can have both negative and positive characteristics *and still* be safe and loving people. This inability to tolerate ambiguity and vulnerability in relationships can lead us to withdraw from the relationship in a type of preemptive strike so that we do not experience those painful feelings of perceived abandonment again.

We also may feel we are constantly on edge in relationships, waiting for the other person to suddenly change their feelings or mood toward us. Even if we do find ourselves in a stable relationship with a healthy and relatively constant person, we still feel deep down that this stability is only temporary, and that at any given moment, if we are not good enough, the relationship could change or dissolve. In an attempt to prevent rejection or the failure of the relationship, we exhibit people-pleaser behavior, which leads us to feel resentful because we have put excessive effort into the relationship, and we secretly expect the other person to do so as well. The resentment can lead to anger and bitterness and can cause us to act in ways that aren't typical for us, throwing others into confusion.

There is also a strong connection between abandonment and betrayal—the two cannot be separated. When a caregiver violates his or her role, a child feels deeply betrayed, and this adds another layer of grief and pain that must be worked through. Just as we can be hypervigilant for abandonment, we can also become hypervigilant for betrayal. We may have a hard time experiencing ordinary disappointments in relationships without feeling like betrayal has again appeared in our lives. Of course, disappointment is the trigger for this distress, but the feelings of betrayal are coming from another time and experience.

Fear of Rejection

Our past experiences with betrayal and abandonment create a fear of rejection. As a result, we tend to end up living our life through the lens or belief system that we will be rejected and abandoned at some point. This colors our perceptions of others, ourselves, and our relationships. We begin to see the world as a place of rejection, and this influences what we pay attention to and how we react to things. It can become the driving force in our lives, and we end up focusing on the negative aspects of relationships, to the exclusion of what is right and positive. This happens because, when we live in a chronic state of hypervigilance, we constantly scan for any danger or threat that we will be rejected or abandoned again. For example, we will often discard positive comments or compliments from another because we deem them "irrelevant," since they are not evidence of a threat or consistent with the negative beliefs we have of ourselves. Hypervigilance is only interested in what is potentially wrong or threatening, never in what is right and good. For example, we could be at an event with others and receive ten positive affirmations, but we will hang on to the one negative, or even just ambiguous, comment more firmly than the rest.

This way of being keeps us trapped in our fear of rejection and abandonment. Hypervigilance is the great thief—it robs us of gratitude, blinds us to the good things in our lives, and steals the present moment from us. It also traps us in a loop and keeps us living out a past wrong. We can only break the loop when we begin to become aware of the hypervigilance and break the cycle of assigning meaning to the negative or ambiguous aspects of interactions and relationships. How to break this cycle is covered in the next two chapters.

Abandonment and Social Situations

The effects of abandonment often show themselves in social situations as well as in our close relationships, albeit in largely nonverbal ways. This is because abandonment and chronic rejection affect our nervous system, which we rely on when we encounter other individuals or we have group interactions. Our nervous system continuously scans our environment for signs of danger and safety, and through it we communicate with nonverbal cues. For example, we can unintentionally send subtle signals to others that we aren't safe to be around. On some level, we are aware of our struggles and fears, so we issue a distress beacon to stay way, to not get too close, because we are in a state of distress and pain. We know relationships are challenging, and in our present state, ours might end badly. We send these nonverbal cues far more often than we realize—sometimes we will simply appear uninterested, quiet, or guarded. Other signals include keeping the conversation short; limiting or constricting our range of emotion; not sustaining eye contact; appearing to be nervous, tense, or overly serious; or not laughing or otherwise engaging in humor. As minor as these cues may seem, they effectively communicate to others, "You stay over there, I'll stay here—don't get too close to me."

Trauma and abandonment aren't the only reasons we send these kinds of signals. Any significantly painful experience that involved some form of hurt or rejection can cause us to broadcast our lack of safety to others. We are in essence trying to prevent others from getting too close to us. *I will disappoint you,* we are telling them. *You will inevitably reject and hurt me; you cannot possibly like or love me for who I am; I have been hurt and I don't have confidence that I can maintain control of this pain.* Of course, these beliefs are not true—we are once again following the script of the distorted and negative beliefs we acquired through painful experiences.

Object Constancy

Our distorted and negative beliefs can also make us feel anxious when people we love and need are not physically present with us—for example, when a loved one goes on a trip, off to college, or stays overnight somewhere. We may notice disproportionate emotional reactions to otherwise ordinary departures, as though the person is leaving forever or has even been lost. Even if we tell ourselves they will only be gone a few days, we feel as though we'll never see them again. Cognitively, we may recognize that the separation is normal, but we can't shake the sense that something unnatural or wrong is happening. We might be able to dismiss these reactions as separation anxiety, but although we expect this in young children, excessive or debilitating separation anxiety is not a healthy sign in adults. In these instances, the separation anxiety is a symptom of the larger issue—namely, unresolved abandonment issues that have affected our ability to cultivate healthy attachments to others.

When we have healthy ways of relating with others, we can maintain an emotional bond with them even if there is conflict or separation through distance. We can generally trust in the resilience of the bond or relationship, and we tend not to swing like a pendulum back and forth between extremes. We also tend to be grounded in our relationships and do not overreact if there is conflict, ambiguity, or distance. This theory of attachment is called object constancy. Object constancy is the emotional version of object permanency, a term coined by the famous developmental psychologist Piaget. Object permanence, a skill we acquire around age two or three, refers to the ability to know that objects continue to exist even if we cannot see or touch them. Object *constancy*, though, involves the ability to preserve an idea of the continued existence of a person even when they are away. We can trust that they still exist, although we cannot see them, and they still maintain a presence in our lives even when we might not have predictable or frequent contact with them. Object constancy also allows us to have a healthy trust and sense of security in ourselves. When we have a healthy degree of object constancy, we don't tend to need the constant affirmation from others that comes through their presence or frequent contact. However, if we struggle with fear of abandonment, our acquisition of object constancy was disrupted and we may therefore lack these abilities.

For many of us, our abandonment wounds occurred when we were very young, although they did not necessarily need to occur in the object permanence phase when we were still preverbal (in the two- to three-year age range) in order to affect us. Even in later childhood, attachment trauma such as this book has been discussing—like having inconsistent caregivers or emotionally unavailable parents—can evoke a fear of abandonment in adulthood and disrupt object constancy. As we have seen, when our fear of abandonment is triggered, the past gets superimposed on the present. We become confused about where we are, and we can feel like a child all over again. Our body is here in the present, but our mind is back in the time and place where we first felt abandonment. We regress to a child state or a child-ego state, and we cannot preserve the idea that a person still exists even when they are away. The feelings that come with abandonment are debilitating. They often include loneliness, emptiness, and the feeling of having a hole or pit in our stomach.

We can also re-experience a profound sense of shame and weakness when these fears are triggered in the present. It would seem counterintuitive to many that the one who was abandoned would feel shame; after all, the abandonment was not their fault. However, to be in need and dependent on another is to be vulnerable, and to be hurt in that vulnerable state and in such a relationship leaves us feeling weak. And many of us feel shame when we feel we are weak. Inevitably, when we experience abandonment, we struggle to assign meaning in order to understand why it happened. Most of us end up making sense of it in a way that is not accurate nor helpful, and we emerge from the abandonment experience believing we are defective and flawed.

When we were young, we may have noticed that we were not protected and taken care of as we should have been. As adults, we can understand that Mom and Dad had major struggles that had nothing to do with us, though we were affected by them. However, the child mind doesn't have the cognitive tools to see or understand the struggles of the parents. As a result, the rejected or abandoned child can blame themselves for the abandonment. Whether this self-blame occurs or not, the one who is abandoned emerges from these experiences deeply believing that they are "damaged goods." They were deprived of the deep affirmation from their parents that they matter and are worth looking after. There is a fundamental loss of self-worth that comes from the realization, "If I was worthwhile, then why did this occur?" And as an adult we can be left with a profound belief that we do not matter. The child emerging from an abandonment experience is left with a deep sense of brokenness that can hang like a shadow over their adult life until it is discovered and resolved. The next chapter will help us learn to uncover these painful and distorted beliefs and to begin the process of revising them.

CHAPTER 5

Discovering Our Cognitive Map

THE NEXT STEP IN OUR healing work is to ask ourselves the question: what have I come to believe because of my life experiences? This question opens a door to our cognitive world and introduces to us to the field and practice of cognitive behavioral therapy (CBT). Cognitive behavioral therapy was founded by Aaron T. Beck in the early 1960s. It was innovative at the time due to its structured, short-term, and goal-oriented approach. Its aim was, and still is, the identification and revision of unhealthy thinking and behavior. It is based on the belief posited by Beck that perception precedes all emotion; we feel how we think. CBT postulates that the negative emotions we struggle with are due to inaccurate and distorted deep-seated beliefs that influence our motivations, thoughts, perceptions, and behaviors.

It is important to note that while CBT can be very helpful in treating anxiety, depression, and phobias, it has not proven effective for *full* recovery from traumatic experiences. If we have suffered from a traumatic experience, CBT can help us mainly in just one stage of our healing work: gaining valuable data about how our experience affected us. It can help us understand exactly how the trauma changed our beliefs about ourselves, others, and the world. It also helps us identify the event or experience of origin that is causing our present distress, and it helps us identify our triggers and what present-day situations are problematic for us. However, when it comes to putting a traumatic past in the past in a very real and experiential way that allows us freedom from the influence of it, CBT has limitations. CBT can certainly give us insight and greater self-awareness, and open us up to having new experiences, which can help us unlearn what we learned from pain in the past. But in light of new knowledge of trauma's effect on the brain, it will not be quite enough to allow us to store traumatic memories away where they need to be stored. More about this will be covered in later chapters.

CBT can help us understand why we struggle in interpersonal relationships. Many of us might feel that our relationships repeat a pattern of experiences where the result is always the same, and we look back on those experiences with only a dim awareness of what occurred. We no doubt had hope for each relationship, and we know the hopes we had were not fulfilled. As a result of these negative experiences, we may feel confused, blame ourselves for what happened, and develop a torrent of negative beliefs about ourselves. Or we may blame others and believe that people will inevitably hurt us. However, if we are willing to do the work presented in this chapter, we can cast a light upon our relationships with both others and ourselves. We can learn exactly why we have struggled and what we need to do to create change and stop the repetitive cycle of painful interactions and perceptions. The following section will cover the two important aspects of core beliefs: conditional or intermediate beliefs, and automatic thoughts. After each concept is explained, you will also learn how to identify how these concepts play out in your own life.

The first step to mapping out our cognitive world is to identify and become familiar with our core beliefs: what we have learned to believe about ourselves, others, and the world in which we live. According to Aaron Beck, there are two categories of core beliefs: those related to unlovability and those related to help-lessness.[1] Our core beliefs begin developing in childhood and continue as we age and have more experiences, but we are often not conscious of them. They may lie dormant and only be acti-vated during a time of stress or a when something triggers us, when they then pulsate to the surface of our conscious mind and affect our thoughts, feelings, and behavior. We can even spend a lifetime never becoming aware of their existence and the role they have played in our lives, even though they may motivate us to spend a lifetime trying to prove to ourselves and others that they are not true. (For some examples of common core beliefs, see Appendix D on page 169.)

When an experience activates a negative core belief, we sud-denly see life through a different lens. One could even say each core belief *is* a lens through which we see and perceive our lives. When the core belief is active, we tend to perceive only that which confirms it. Anything that contradicts that negative core belief we dismiss or only briefly retain. To better understand this, imagine someone who has a core belief that they are "not good enough." When that person is complimented or praised, they will either immediately dismiss the compliment or hold onto it for

---

1 Judith S. Beck, *Cognitive Behavior Therapy, Third Edition: Basics and Beyond* (New York: The Guilford Press, 2020), 26.

only a brief time, quickly forgetting it as other experiences that support the negative core belief then record over it.

A good analogy for those who have been chronically de-validated, criticized, and locked in self-blame is what occurs when we gaze at the sun. We can only glance for a moment because the glare causes us to turn away. This is the effect that affirmations and praise can have on those who have negative core beliefs as a result of being treated negatively. Affirmations cause an emotional glare in the form of incongruence. Though the affirmation is positive, it is not what we have known of ourselves. We cannot reconcile the two, so we eventually dismiss the positive thoughts or feedback in order to preserve our negative self-image. However, if someone gets upset at us, we do not get the results we expected, or we receive anything close to criticism, we immediately hold onto that experience and assimilate it into our perception. This is akin to looking up at the sky on a cloudy day—there is no glare and therefore no need to turn away. For those of us who have been verbally and emotionally cut down or trapped in the shame of self-blame, negative experiences do cause distress. But there is a familiarity to them and a type of soothing as we get reinforcement for what we have believed about ourselves for so long.

Core beliefs can form gradually over time or quickly from acute experiences. In the former, having chronic repetitive experiences that result in the same feelings can cause the formation of a negative core belief. When we are not conscious of what is occurring, we are not able to realize that our repetitive negative experience is only tied to a *particular* situation, relationship, or person. Instead, we gradually identify in a very general way with this interaction and let it lead to overall and absolute perceived truths about ourselves. However, once we become more familiar with CBT, we can prevent the formation of negative core beliefs by learning to catch ourselves and reframe and revise the meaning we assign to interactions and experiences. This also applies to negative core beliefs that form from an acute experience. When the acute experience is over, we can learn to reframe what occurred and begin to prevent certain beliefs from forming because of the experience. This will be covered later in this chapter.

Katherine: A Case Study

Katherine was a thirty-seven-year-old single woman who never married. She worked as a full-time teacher and did well at her job. She got along well with her fellow teachers and the school staff, so long as the interactions stayed on the professional or more superficial level. However, she noticed that whenever she attempted to have a closer relationship with someone, a particular set of struggles would occur. After so many years, Katherine could look back and see several relationships that could have been good friendships, but these struggles disrupted them. After many years of these repetitive experiences, she developed a default strategy of maintaining distance from others in order to stop the same things from happening again. This led to loneliness and a growing realization that without help, she was on a trajectory to spend the rest of her life alone. As we so often see, such ways of coping are not sustainable in the long run, as they will inevitably just inflict more pain and suffering.

Katherine sought out counseling to help her finally understand and resolve what was happening. Through the course of the counseling, Katherine learned to see the patterns in her struggles. She learned there was a common theme to her thoughts when she interacted with others, and she learned to identify a certain feeling that tended to be present when she ventured into relationships. Additionally, she learned there was a common fear operating behind all her interactions.

She also identified the first time she could remember feeling this way. When she was young, she lived in a chronic state of uncertainty in regard to her parents' feelings toward her. Katherine's relationship with her parents was one of ambiguity. One day they were pleased with her, and the next day they were not, due to something she did that they thought was not good enough. Thus, Katherine felt profoundly rejected by her parents and ashamed of her behavior. She had learned to believe that she was unlovable, unworthy, not good enough, and ultimately that she disappoints others.

Katherine, with the help of the counselor, learned to identify core beliefs she had developed that lay at the heart of her struggles. And as counseling continued, she began to learn how these core beliefs drove her behavior, motives, and choices. She also learned that the core beliefs that had developed through the way her parents treated her extended to her beliefs about others, such as in her belief that other people would reject her and that they are not safe.

Conditional/Intermediate Beliefs

Our core beliefs never really stay stagnant; they pulsate through us from the unconscious, influence our thoughts and motives, and affect our present-day behavior. Though they are largely unconscious, something we can never quite articulate, they drive our motives and behavior. And they inevitably lead us to develop ways of coping with them. These learned dispositions or ways of coping with core beliefs are called conditional or intermediate beliefs. These are the rules, attitudes, or assumptions we develop in response to a core belief—our attempts to cope, avoid the feelings associated with the beliefs, or prove to ourselves and others that those negative core beliefs are not true. Our attempts to cope can be a major culprit behind negative behavior and even lead to self-medication and addiction, and we may learn to live as though we are trying to acquit ourselves of a crime or accusation of which we are not guilty. Our core beliefs can create a minefield of triggers that many people in our present life will inadvertently activate.

To understand how these conditional beliefs work in real life, image how a core belief of "I am incompetent" may lead to interpreting that belief as, "If I can't do everything well, then I am a failure." From this point, we will likely choose one of two options or ways of coping (or fluctuate between both). On the one hand, we may avoid any situation or activity where the negative core belief ("I am incompetent") could become known to others. On the other hand, we may pressure ourselves to unceasingly prove that we are competent. In this instance, our conditional belief would be, "If I try this and don't do well, then everyone will see that I am not good enough." Also, if we choose to cope with that negative core belief by constantly putting too much pressure on ourselves, we likely have no clear marker or accomplishment that, once reached, will give us what we are seeking. In essence, our efforts will be like trying to satisfy our thirst with salt water. No matter how well we do, how much we accomplish, or how much praise we receive from others, it will never be enough. We become our own taskmaster, not allowing ourselves any rest. This is because the negative core belief still exists and has not been revised.

If we have a core belief that we are incompetent or not good enough, any accomplishments, praise, and affirmations from others will offer us relief and satisfaction only in the short-term. Soon the unconscious drive kicks in again and we set out on the exhausting quest to eliminate the negative core belief by trying to prove it wrong. This quest can become like our own pursuit of the white whale from the famous tale *Moby Dick*. The disruption from the negative core belief, and subsequent conditional belief, can rob us of joy and peace in our lives. It can also prevent us from being in the present moment and take us away from those we are closest to. The impulse for revising a negative core belief and giving up the conditional belief that drives our motives and behavior must come from within, not from without. It is only when we become conscious of the core belief, its origin, and how we have been coping with it, that we can give up the destructive and exhausting quest to prove something that does not need to be proven. (For more examples of common conditional beliefs, please see Appendix D, page 170.)

Case Study: Katherine's Healing Work Continues

As Katherine continued counseling and working on herself between sessions, she learned that she had developed certain ways of coping with her core beliefs. Only then could she begin to see how and why she struggled in relationships. She recognized her conditional beliefs and became aware that she had been living with the belief that if she could accomplish or prove certain things, she would not experience again what she had in her past. One by one, both in session and in her notebook, she identified the conditional belief for each respective core belief. In response to the core belief that people will reject her, she had developed the conditional belief of "If only I work hard enough, no one will reject me." In response to the core belief that she is defective, she had developed the conditional belief, "If I avoid close relationships, no one will see that I am broken."

While it was a great relief for Katherine to gain awareness of these beliefs that had been operating, she also felt grief over the realization that she had been living like this for so long. She allowed herself to feel empathy for herself over what she had experienced in her home growing up and how it had affected her so deeply, showing the same compassion for herself she would have shown to someone else with similar experiences. She now had to begin letting go of the behaviors on which she had been expending so much time and energy. Keeping others at a distance, she now realized, had only reinforced her perception that she was broken and defective. She and her counselor began to create homework assignments where she would have to step out of her comfort zone and begin initiating social activities with others. She also had to let go of her workaholic work style that was driven by her need to please others in order to avoid rejection.

Automatic Thoughts: How We Dialogue with Ourselves

So far, we have covered the presence of negative core beliefs and how they lead to the formation of dispositions as we try to cope with them. Automatic thoughts also affect how we cope with core beliefs. These are simply the stream of thoughts that pass through our mind throughout the day. We usually are not conscious of them, and they are often heavily influenced by our core beliefs, our conditional beliefs, and the dispositions we live by.

Our automatic thoughts have a significant impact on our emotions. We would all readily agree that when our thoughts are negative in nature, we feel lousy, but that when our thoughts are positive, we feel better. This seems quite simple and even self-evident. No doubt we have all said to ourselves, "Why am I so negative?" or others have pointed this out to us. There is always a reason behind an inclination toward negative thinking, whether it is just a temporary episode or we experiencing it chronically. We can use our automatic thoughts to help us uncover our more deeply rooted core beliefs and conditional beliefs or dispositions. We can also use our core beliefs and conditional beliefs to help us become more aware of our automatic thoughts and where they are coming from.

One exercise that can help is to sit with a piece of paper and write down the stream of thoughts that passes through our mind daily. We will begin to see a general theme or trend to them. Looking at them closely, we see that they indicate certain beliefs we have of others, ourselves, the world, and even God. This helps us identify our core beliefs: If I often think negative thoughts about myself, then what do I believe about myself? If I have chronic negative thoughts about others, then what do I believe about other people in general? If I have negative thoughts about life in general and the world, then what do I believe about my life and the larger world? Once we have identified our core beliefs, we can then explore how we have coped with our negative beliefs and perceptions. What have we been trying to prove or avoid in our lives? There is always an answer. This leads us to our conditional beliefs or dispositions. Our negative core beliefs never stay silent. They drive and determine many of our motives, thoughts, and behaviors.

Another way to identify and become more aware of our daily stream of thoughts is, if we have first identified our core beliefs, to work forward from there. For example, if we know we have a negative core belief that we are defective or not good enough, we would look for the presence of thoughts that typically take the form of "I am a fake," "I hate myself," "I can't do anything right," and "Why would someone want to be around me?" These thoughts are only a few of many types of thoughts that might emanate from such a core belief. (For more examples of types of automatic thoughts, see Appendix D, page 171.)

Sometimes we are aware of automatic thoughts, but usually we are not. They often pass as soon as they enter our mind. Yet even when they come and go quickly, they inflict their sting and hurt and damage our mood. These thoughts can also cause a sudden change in mood. A situation can activate a negative core belief and trigger a cascade of negative thoughts, and we can suddenly find our mood spiraling downward. We then find ourselves feeling profoundly depressed or anxious, filled with sadness or fear.

Sometimes these thoughts do not just pass through, and we hold onto them and use them to beat ourselves up. If we suffer from shame and self-loathing, we even almost *like* to beat up on ourselves because it is what we know. Also, sometimes when burdened by too much emotional baggage, we become emotionally numb, and we like to inflict ourselves with negative thoughts because at least we are feeling something—even if it is guilt, shame, and self-loathing.

Many of us are not aware of how we can perpetuate our struggle through our thoughts, though there is great truth to the adage that we feel how we think. We speak now of how we relate with ourselves, that is, our inner disposition. We all have an inner dialogue that we maintain, and often we shame ourselves with negative thoughts without realizing it. We cut ourselves down, criticize ourselves, reject ourselves, and express self-hatred. We abuse ourselves. For those of us who have been verbally or emotionally abused at some point in our lives, it is not uncommon that long after the abuser is gone and the abuse has ceased, without realizing it, we continue the abuse by abusing ourselves. We often then do not understand why we are not feeling better. Little do we realize that we have taken the place of the abuser.

Our abusive thoughts can cause us to struggle with depression for many years and even reach the point of believing we cannot change. But once we become aware of our inner dialogue with ourselves and how we relate with ourselves in an abusive way, a powerful opportunity for change and healing becomes available. We then set about stopping the self-abuse. This letting go takes time and practice; however, the effects and benefits are often dramatic. We can go from years of significant depression to suddenly feeling much brighter and cheerful within weeks. Inevitably, we will slip up at times and cut ourselves down with negative or shaming statements. However, it is important that when this occurs, we apologize to ourselves and resolve to not do it anymore. This sends a profound message. We learn to give ourselves the treatment we should have received but did not. We learn that we cannot wait for certain people to come back and treat us differently, to meet those unmet needs; it is just not going to happen. We must meet those needs ourselves by giving ourselves the self-compassion, empathy, mercy, and affirmation we never received. We do this not to become prideful but to heal, so we can become who we would have been had the painful experiences not occurred. We quickly learn that one of our greatest enemies in healing is self-abuse. When we become aware of the self-abuse that was taking place through our automatic thoughts, cease the abuse, apologize to ourselves, and begin to give affirmation and self-compassion to ourselves, the transformation that can occur is profound.

Case Study: The Fruits of Katherine's Healing Work

Katherine began to become more aware of her thoughts— thoughts she had previously dismissed as meaningless, harmless, and fleeting now became targets of change. Katherine was glad to have something concrete to focus on. She did have to come to terms with the realization that she would not receive the statements of affirmation she craved from her parents and from others. The affirmation she so craved and needed would have to come from herself. Katherine began to monitor her thoughts more and learned to catch herself as soon as she would slip up and engage in abusive, negative thoughts about herself. She also learned to apologize to that younger part of herself each time a slipup occurred.

Katherine also continued to become more aware of her triggers. Each trigger that had previously caused so much distress became an opportunity for Katherine to respond differently. She soon became adept at catching herself when beginning a downward spiral of negative thoughts after an ambiguous interaction or when she felt rejected. Katherine was able to respond with more constructive thoughts and show herself encouragement, affirmation, and gentleness. She began to notice she was feeling less depressed, and her self-confidence began to soar. She felt more cheerful and lighthearted. She also noticed that she was more engaged in social interactions and more social, generally, because she was spending less time and energy worrying about the danger of rejection.

Appraisals and the Meanings We Assign

The previous section enabled us to understand why mood changes happen; now we can learn how to prevent the unneeded struggles that mood changes bring by learning what meanings we assign to our experiences. We are always assigning meaning, often unconsciously, and the ability to become aware of what meanings we assign to events, interactions, and the words of others is critical because this helps us stop the emotional downward spiral. The appraisals we make, and the meanings we assign to details of our experiences, are the result of our core beliefs. It is the way our negative core beliefs trickle down to our everyday consciousness. To many this might seem obvious; however, most people pay little attention to the meanings they assign to their many experiences and how those meanings affect their emotional states.

Assigning meanings is typically an automatic process until we gain more insight and have greater familiarity with these concepts. As a result, when we assign negative meaning to a situation where the meaning results from a negative core belief, we often can find ourselves on a downward trajectory emotionally. In order to identify and challenge the meanings we assign to our everyday experiences, we need to make a habit of stopping ourselves and engaging the process when we do experience an abrupt change in mood. We learn to troubleshoot ourselves and say, "Okay, why did my mood just take a dive?" Then we pinpoint the experience that immediately preceded the mood change and find the trigger. Was it a word someone said, someone else's mood or affect, their behavior, or was it something that did not occur that we hoped would occur? Once we pinpoint the trigger, we then ask ourselves what meaning we assigned to it. This leads to a critical and very helpful exercise called the downward arrow technique.

We often assign layers of meanings, and the downward arrow technique is a useful tool to help us peel back the layers and identify which core belief was operating or activated due to the trigger. By using the downward arrow technique, we can get to the core belief or fear that is causing us so much distress. When we do this successfully, it can bring us much relief because we are able to understand exactly why we struggled and where the emotions were coming from. When we develop the ability to troubleshoot our own emotions, it becomes a major confidence booster: we feel more in control and less overwhelmed. We feel more grounded and less fearful of our emotions, and we have greater confidence in our ability to manage, navigate, and master our emotional world. Troubleshooting also brings us greater emotional stability. However, the downward arrow technique requires us to lean into our emotions, rather than avoid them.

We begin by identifying the situation or event that occurred. We then ask ourselves questions. However, the starting question can take different forms. We can start by asking ourselves what meaning we assigned to the situation. "Why did that (the triggering situation) upset me; what did it mean to me?" We then answer our own question with a statement such as, "It upset me because it meant that _____". We then respond, "And if it meant that, then what would that mean?" We can also get more specific and respond, "Then what would it mean about me?" Once we answer, then we respond again, "And if that were true, then that would mean what?" We continue to do this until we cannot go any further, and we sense we have gotten to the core fear or meaning assigned. The core meaning or fear is often concise and resonates with us emotionally. Typically, we will recognize it when we get to it. (To complete this exercise, see Exercise 3: Downward Arrow Exercise in Appendix D, page 172.)

Oftentimes, when we start this exercise, we respond by identifying feelings instead of the meaning we assigned to something. But this exercise seeks the beliefs or meanings assigned, not the emotions: we seek the beliefs or meanings that *drive* our emotions. Each series of questions leads us deeper into our unconscious mind. As we successfully answer each series, each layer of the unconscious mind suddenly becomes the conscious mind. We become archaeological excavators of our mind by bringing the light of the present to the layers of the unresolved past.

As we continue to employ this technique and understand our inner world better, we will increasingly feel that we have fewer unknown parts of ourselves, and we become more confident in our ability to problem solve our emotional world.

Once we are aware of and understand how our thoughts and beliefs affect our perceptions and behaviors, we will need to identify where we learned these negative beliefs. Many of us will know right away or at least have a strong inkling. Others may have a moment of sudden realization because of the insights gained from this chapter. To heal, we do have to come to terms with the causes and origins of our struggles. Once we have identified our core beliefs, we will have to ask ourselves, "Where did I learn to believe this?" If we have a hard time answering this question, we can ask ourselves to identify what we feel when we reflect on that belief or when that belief is triggered. Once we identify those feelings, we then ask ourselves, "When is the first time I remember feeling this way?" The answer to this question very often leads us to the origin of the negative beliefs. This part of the work is not to be the proverbial blame game. We are not interested in the causes for the sake of blame, but for healing and resolution. We might find that the origins of our negative beliefs came from relationships that are still active. This can cause much confusion and incongruence.

Not only does CBT offer insights into our thoughts and beliefs, it also provides behavioral or experiential activities to help us unlearn the negative thoughts and beliefs. Once we become familiar with how to break down and understand our thought processes, we can begin to see the unhealthy behaviors that we learned and developed. We see that our long-standing behavioral patterns, which resulted from our negative and distorted thoughts and beliefs, actually reinforce negative beliefs that we learned earlier in our lives. However, so long as we stay in these guarded or avoidant states, others cannot get close, and we then deprive ourselves of the opportunity to have deep, positive experiences that could help us unlearn our negative beliefs. Our negative core beliefs set us up for self-defeating behaviors. Much of these behaviors are fear driven: we are avoiding a certain feared scenario or outcome. This leads us to the need for learning to rewrite our belief system and override the fear system of our brain. Indeed, our life story is still being written, and our ability to change it is quite powerful.

CHAPTER 6

Healing the Brain

F OR MANY, WHAT HAS SO far been discussed will be enough to create change and bring relief. However, some of us may find only fleeting relief. In other words, we have become more insightful, we have greater understanding of our life experiences and how they have affected us, we may witness an improvement in our relationships and interactions, and we may even feel a greater sense of peace. We might even feel better for several months and assume we have been healed or "cured." However, eventually we begin to struggle again, though perhaps not in the same way as before. It might not be as bad or debilitating this time, as though we have resolved part of the challenge but not all of it. We feel that perhaps we have missed something, which can be frustrating. *What went wrong?* we may wonder. *What did I miss?* After a while we may observe that it is not so much that something has gone wrong but that we have arrived at another layer of healing work that needs attention.

Healing work can be mysterious. We heal in layers, or even piece by piece. We often reach plateaus in this journey, feeling better for a time—after some discovery or breakthrough—and believing that was it, we did it, our work is done. These plateaus often serve as a "breather" or pause in our healing work. They can afford time to rest or assimilate the work we have done so far. But everyone heals differently. For some of us, we can only address the deeper layers after we have resolved the layers closer to the surface. Others of us may skip through the layers to core issues of our struggle, especially if we have reached a crisis point. Either way, we will eventually know when we have reached the core issue. We know it and recognize it, though we hadn't before, as if we had been with someone for a long time without realizing who they really were. Perhaps we had previously caught sight of the core issue but were not yet ready to acknowledge the reality it represented. Or maybe someone else in our lives once brought it to our attention, but it did not resonate at that time because we had other work we needed to do first.

This often happens when we are suffering from an unresolved traumatic experience in our lives. As mentioned earlier, many of our struggles may be resolved from what has so far been discussed. However, when it comes to healing from trauma, long-lasting and permanent healing will not come from insight, self-discovery, and talking alone. No doubt, many of us may groan upon this realization, while others may feel relieved that there is a reason we are still struggling, other than some personal failing. We may have spent many years talking about our experience, shedding tears, grieving, and journaling, yet find we are still reacting in the same way to triggers. We simply can't seem to shake certain disproportionate emotional reactions to certain situations. It is normal to feel a mixture of emotion when we realize that what we thought was healing was just a temporary break in our healing work, and now we must make a final push to reach that summit of resolution.

Memory and Trauma

The reason insight, self-discovery, grieving, and journaling are often not enough is because trauma affects all areas of the brain. Therefore, healing from traumatic experiences requires using all areas of our brain. Some basic understanding of how traumatic experiences affect the brain and memory is critical. The accumulation of memories and our mind's assimilation of them is what leads to our external sense of reality, but trauma causes a breakdown in memory formation. Normal memories are integrated fully, and our external sense of reality is flexible and malleable in the face of new incoming information and experiences that we have in our present, everyday lives. We adapt, adjust, and grow throughout our lives. At least, this is what is supposed to happen. But at the core of all trauma is a profound sense of violation and betrayal that is so strong it shuts down certain aspects of memory storage and causes us to feel trapped in the past. Trauma is the most extreme form of incongruence our minds can encounter. When we have been traumatized, we have suffered an injury so grievous to our mind and soul, it disrupts the narrative and flow of our lives because it keeps us stuck and frozen at the time of the trauma.

To further understand how this happens, we need to delve deeper into how memory works. Dr. Peter Levine has used what is known about the different kinds of memory to understand just how traumatic experiences affect our learning and behavior.[2]

2   Peter A. Levine, *Trauma and Memory: Brain and Body in a Search for the Living Past: A Practical Guide for Understanding and Working with Traumatic Memory* (Berkeley, CA: North Atlantic Books, 2015), 37.

We have two types of memory: explicit and implicit. Explicit memory, also called declarative memory, is that which we can readily recall. Implicit memory is our unconscious memory. We cannot access it as easily as explicit memory; however, it greatly influences our emotions and behavior. Both types contain two further subsets or types of memory. Explicit memory has two subsets: autobiographical, or episodic, memory and semantic memory. Episodic memory can be readily accessed or triggered by an experience; however, we know and understand the process. We can see or experience someone or something, and suddenly become nostalgic or reminiscent. Semantic memory simply involves our knowledge of basic facts and general knowledge.

The two subsets of implicit memory, which can often be the most disrupted if trauma has occurred in our lives, are known as emotional and procedural memory. Emotional memory is when we can readily feel emotions associated with a past event when something in the present reminds us of that event. In other words, when emotional memory is activated, we feel the emotions of memories. Such experiences often feel disproportionate, and we feel baffled as to why we had such a powerful reaction. Procedural memory is the knowledge we use to do tasks. It is the memory we use to ride a bike, drive a car, or navigate stairs. It is functional memory.

Trauma can affect both types of memories and all four of the subsets because it causes a breakdown of the normal memory system. During a traumatic experience, the prefrontal cortex, which has been called the "time-keeping" part of the brain, can shut down. As a result, a traumatic experience takes on a timeless quality. It becomes something of the past, present, and future.

This is one reason why we feel as though we cannot simply get over or move past a traumatic experience. So, a traumatic memory is one that is not integrated normally. When a memory is integrated normally, its context as a past memory is understood. However, with a traumatic memory, we cannot tell whether a memory is from the past or the present. Cognitively, we may be able to identify it as a past experience; however, our emotional memory (a subset of implicit memory) holds it as though it is an active and present experience. When we have had a traumatic experience, it is as though we keep following a past story and rereading it in a never-ending loop. Though time has moved on and we continue to have new experiences, the traumatic memory that has not been integrated acts as our interpreter of present events, as a story of the past that gets superimposed on the present. It causes us to confuse the present with the past. Trauma is an isolated past experience that keeps pushing its way to the present. This is precisely why, in such cases, talking and insight alone are not enough to bring us durable and genuine healing from a traumatic experience.

Our procedural memory (another subset of implicit memory) is also impacted by traumatic experiences.[3] Procedural learning is a normal and necessary process that helps us know how to function in the world. For example, we learn through experience how to do very common tasks, such as making a deposit at the bank or putting Christmas lights on a tree. In these instances, what we are taught is positive. Also, because these experiences result in non-traumatic memories, our brain integrates them normally. Therefore, they are flexible and adaptive, should they need to be

---

3 Levine, *Trauma and Memory*, 25.

changed. For example, because those memories were processed and stored normally, should we find out new data that indicates there is a better way to make the bank deposit or decorate the Christmas tree, we are able to readily and easily change how we do it the next time.

However, how does procedural learning work when a traumatic experience happens? Tragically, trauma also creates new procedural memories. It creates new ways for us to think, function, relate, and respond that were born from an experience where there was a terrible threat or betrayal. They are formed from our attempts to survive that experience. Then, because of the timeless nature of traumatic memories, those procedural memories do not go away but stay active long after the traumatic experience has concluded. So, at the time of the trauma, we may have learned certain coping behaviors to survive the experience. However, when the experience is over, we continue to cope and function the same way. We can see how this causes much disruption and grief in our lives. Also, due to the timelessness of the traumatic memory and its incomplete integration, we cannot adjust to present experiences that tell us that the way we are acting, in response to this memory, is harmful.

Additionally, we not only remember the memory, we feel it. Our body carries memory through physical sensations and our body language. So, in addition to the verbal narrative of our painful experiences, there is something called our somatic narrative, which is the story that our body tells.[4] Our somatic narrative

---

4 Pat Ogden, Kekuni Minton, and Clare Pain, *Trauma and the Body: A Sensorimotor Approach to Psychotherapy* (New York: W. W. Norton & Company, 2006), 229.

is how we hold ourselves, and it reveals how we feel the painful experience—so the body itself, its presentation, gives us a glimpse into our past. Our somatic narrative is our posture, facial expression, affect, cadence, tone of voice, walk, and even our breathing. Whether of ourselves or of someone else, we must learn to ask, does our verbal narrative match our somatic narrative? Our body language, expression, and posture are like the pictures in our life story, and our verbal details are the words on the page.[5] We need to make sure they are congruent.

We may have been denying our struggles, our painful experiences, and their effects on us for many years. And in doing so, we told ourselves a story. However, our body may be telling us a different story—that is, the real story. This is not because we are being dishonest; sometimes we are just not ready to acknowledge what has occurred in our lives. Sometimes, we attempt to sweep experiences under the proverbial carpet because they are just too painful. Or we might not be consciously aware or may have suppressed awareness of a traumatic experience. However, our body always tells the story. The unconscious mind speaks through our body, through our somatic narrative and symptoms: we are getting a glimpse of our nervous system through our body. So, when our somatic narrative shows evidence of being stuck in a negative or frozen state, it is in essence showing us the state we were in while the trauma was occurring.

A major paradigm shift in the treatment of trauma involves

---

5   Ruth Buczynski, *Treating Trauma Master Series*, with Bessel van der Kolk, et al., Online Training Module (National Institute for the Clinical Application of Behavioral Medicine), https://www.nicabm. com/confirm/treating-trauma-master-2/.

first working with the effects of the trauma, not the memories. But inevitably, there are instances when we cannot recall our trauma, though it is clear something occurred. Addressing the somatic narrative by focusing on a certain physical symptom or sensation can help bring to the surface memories we had completely forgotten or suppressed. While this approach does not focus on the memories themselves, having some idea of what occurred is helpful. But we sometimes can place too much pressure on ourselves to remember, to recall every detail. It is natural to want to remember and recall details, and we should not be discouraged from this; however, our primary focus should be on the *effects* of our painful experience rather than the details.

Beyond Talk Therapy and the Life Story

Research into the idea of focusing on the somatic narrative, on the *effects* of trauma instead of on memories, has shown that in general, talk therapy alone will not help get our nervous system unstuck, and neither will insight and self-discovery by themselves. Creating a narrative or life story is still important for insight and to help us see the proverbial forest for the trees in our lives. And we still benefit when we tell our story. We get to experience someone listening to us, we receive empathy, and we release a secret. However, verbally telling or writing our story will not be enough to bring us to full healing. Revising our negative beliefs is also not enough. No matter how often we tell our story and do the cognitive work, it will not stop the body from feeling the traumatic experience. Also, the repetitive telling of our story beyond what is helpful can be exhausting and lead to frustration when we wonder why we are still not feeling better. It serves a purpose early in our healing work but can be unproductive if we rely on it alone to heal from profoundly painful or traumatic experiences.

To heal from a frozen nervous system that is still guarding against threats, we need to use the same parts of the brain that were traumatized, and talk therapy alone does not access all affected parts of the brain. We will need treatment that is more experiential: that is, based on having new experiences. (For those who feel reticent to participate in talk therapy, this is welcome news.) When we think of experiential treatment, we might think of the stereotypical hitting of pillows or some other object. We now know that those old techniques are not helpful because when we try to get our anger out by kicking or hitting things, we enter a dissociative state. We check out and go somewhere else as our focus and attention become myopic, blocking out our surrounding environment. Once again, just as with talk therapy alone, we are only using one or too few parts of the brain. We will need to have experiences that activate the same parts of the brain as the traumatic experience.

This takes us back to how trauma is held in the body and manifests itself through unpleasant feelings and bodily sensations. Those who specialize in helping people heal from trauma now believe that trauma lies not so much in the mind but in the body. Many of the leading experts in the field report that they don't need to hear the verbal narrative of what happened; they just need to know where we feel it in our body. So, if we were to seek help from someone well trained and current with the latest knowledge, they would likely ask us not to tell our story but to say where we feel the unpleasant feelings in our body. When we engage in this work, we will be asked to report where we feel it in our body when we think of a painful memory, fear, or image. They will also ask us what happens to our body when we allow ourselves to sit with the memories, fears, or images. We take big steps in healing by focusing on these sensations that we have so long avoided, until we eventually become okay with them and no longer feel threatened by them or fear and dread them. Once this desensitization to the feared feeling occurs, we are no longer troubled by the memories or awareness of the experience.

To begin to go deeper into our healing work, it helps us to become more attuned to the unpleasant feelings in our body that trauma creates. When we have had a traumatic experience, we tend to feel it in the middle section of our body, such as in the gut area. Until we get the relief we need, we are prone to some form of self-medicating in an attempt to manage the emotional pain and bodily sensations. We may self-medicate with food, drugs, alcohol, gambling, sexual activity, or compulsive buying. We may also be prone to dissociating or find ourselves feeling emotionally numb, and we tend to avoid negative feelings. Learning to not engage in emotional avoidance is a key part of healing from traumatic experiences. In fact, some leading researchers believe that once we can be at peace with and tolerate the negative feelings and sensations associated with a traumatic experience, we have no need to do any further work. This will result in the healing we need.

Whether our negative experiences were traumatic or just profoundly disappointing, we also often feel helpless and weak because we were frozen at the moment of our most profoundly painful experiences. Even if it was just for a moment, we were still at the mercy of someone or something else's actions. Finding ways to reverse this frozen state is critical in healing, and to do so, we will need to have experiences that contradict the messages of the body, or our somatic narrative. Bessel van der Kolk explains that trauma lies in our automatic reactions and dispositions, and in how we interpret the world. To heal, we must rewire these automatic perceptions by having deep experiences that contradict what our traumatic experience taught us.[6]

The cognitive behavioral therapy work we may have done can be very useful here because we may already know what negative beliefs we learned because of our painful experience. However, it is not enough to simply tell ourselves these beliefs are not true; we must *experience* that they are not true. But because of our painful experiences, we tend to be unable to have the very experiences we need to heal. When we have had a traumatic or profoundly painful experience, our world shrinks. We withdraw from others and from life, and we can develop a guarded disposition and not allow others to get close. This is because we are afraid. We were hurt and we fear being hurt again, so our nervous system stays stuck in this defensive posture. This short-term (albeit understandable) way of coping hurts us in the long run and keeps us stuck because we are not able to have new experiences that override the survival part of the brain.

This leads us to the concept of neural plasticity, which is the nervous system's ability to change and reorganize through new experiences. Previously it had been believed that such changes could only occur when we were in our early developmental stages,

---

6 Buczynski, *Treating Trauma Master Series*, "How to Work with the Limbic System to Reverse the Physiological Imprint of Trauma."

but now we know that the nervous system has the ability to make structural changes due to our needs throughout our lives. The two core processes that drive our neural plasticity are learning and behavior. When we have experiences, we create memories. Our memories are made up of neural networks, which is a network of neurons. When trauma occurs, groups of neurons, especially those related to protection and survival, can start to connect more strongly with each other while becoming more isolated from the rest of the brain. As a result, these neural networks can get stuck and resist taking in new information. For example, long after a painful experience, we may continue to suffer from shame and the feeling of being unsafe, even if we find ourselves surrounded by people and activities that do the opposite of shaming and are quite safe. However, these experiences can't change the learning that took place in response to the painful experience because we are unable to process the new information. This is because the new information contradicts our learned negative beliefs and because the neural networks that formed were not integrated fully and were somewhat detached from the rest of our memory. It is almost as though we will not give ourselves permission to believe and accept what our present life is telling us. We are cooperating with our trauma response and living a life that is fear-driven and focused on perceived survival.

Limbic System Therapy

Van der Kolk also speaks about a type of therapy he calls limbic system therapy.[7] It is not so much a formal type of therapy as it is a focus on healing activities that target the limbic system,

---

7   Buczynski, "How to Work with the Limbic System."

the part of the brain that controls our behavioral and emotional responses—especially the ones we utilize for survival, including our fight-or-flight response. Limbic system therapy involves allowing ourselves, and creating for ourselves, deep experiences that make us believe we are not always helpless and unsafe. It helps us find activities that give us the opportunity for deep experiences that contradict the somatic narrative and the inner disposition that we learned from our painful experience(s). Our painful or traumatic experiences are deep, and so our healing experiences need to be deep and meaningful. These new meaningful experiences afforded by limbic system therapy allow us to feel affirmed and loved. They need to be empowering and healing, and ultimately give us the deep belief that we can do things we had never thought possible due to our painful or traumatic experience. Van der Kolk describes these experiences as designed to override the lessons our body and nervous system learned during our traumatic or profoundly painful experience. For these new experiences to override the safety part of the brain, they need to be significant enough. This means we will have to put ourselves out there, so to speak. We will need to go significantly beyond our comfort zones, which have shrunk due to our experiences. Also, to have these deep experiences and override our protective dispositions, we first will have to give ourselves permission to do something different and to embrace the positive feelings and beliefs these different experiences create. There is a synergy that is needed because in turn, as we have these deep, positive experiences, we will need to be open to and accepting of what they teach us. For many this might seem self-evident. However, when we have been accustomed to relating a certain way for so long, it is not so easy; we will need to be deliberate in giving ourselves permission to change how we relate with ourselves and others.

An example of such a healing experience is being part of a community—not just through membership but through participation. To go further, it is not just through participation but also through deep connections with those in the community. This is especially true if our painful or traumatic experience occurred in the context of a relationship. Our painful experience taught us that relationships are intrinsically not safe, that deep connections are a vulnerability we can ill afford, and that overall, all relationships are a source of danger and of potentially re-experiencing our past experiences. If it is through a relationship that our hurt occurred, then it is through relationships that we will need to be healed. God heals, of course, but there also has to be synergy—we must do our part. If we stay stuck in the trauma response that tells us relationships are inherently dangerous, how will we ever be able to love and be loved?

Another example of a healing act that can override the safety part of our brain is when we initiate social contact. Rather than waiting to see if others reach out, we begin to reach out. We will feel discomfort in this, and we will need to tolerate the discomfort and push through it. There is always the chance that when we initiate social contact it may not go as we hope, but even this is a perfect opportunity when we use it to practice other interpretations other than what our past painful or traumatic experiences taught us. We can try again with someone else, and suddenly, rather than being passive and helpless, we become empowered. We can act, we can move and engage. We are no longer sitting passively, watching life go by like a deer in the headlights, and we are no longer stuck in a trauma response, for we are moving on and engaging the present and not the past. It is difficult to do in the beginning; however, it does not take long for our confidence to grow, for those neural pathways to change, and for our trauma response to become something of the past. Of course, this takes time, and we must move slowly and not rush ourselves. It is important for us to be patient and gentle with ourselves as we engage in the act of unfreezing time and nudge our nervous system back to the present.

Any activity or newly learned skill such as these builds confidence and helps us know, feel, and believe that we can do things we had not thought we could when we were still stuck emotionally. In other words, we begin living the life we would have had if the traumatic or painful experience had not happened. We certainly keep the positive aspects or the silver lining we might have gained from our past experiences. However, what about the positive things we might have experienced but did not? We can now set about pursuing those things, and as we live more lovingly and boldly, our minds experience relationships and activities that might have similar settings to where our hurt or trauma occurred, but this time they are on our terms and with a different outcome. Instead of betrayal, rejection, or injury, we experience love, affirmation, belonging, and confidence. And as new neural pathways are created and written, our fear responses lessen, and we become unstuck.

As we actively continue to engage our life narrative through the present, our somatic narrative changes as well. The face that was once tense begins to loosen and smile. The rigid shoulders begin to relax. Our cadence of voice changes and becomes less monotone. Our affect expands and brightens. We move more, and we have a greater range of emotion. Our gait may change, become lighter, and have a spring to it. We may have better color in our face. These are all beautiful signs that our nervous system is returning to the present. Our nervous system also begins to send out messages to others that we are open for business, that we are no longer unsafe to be around. The nonverbal and unconscious distress signal we unknowingly emitted to others becomes silent, for it no longer serves a purpose. We have rejoined humanity of the present rather than of the past. We are no longer at risk of being left behind by time due to our traumatic or painful experience. As the trauma response fades, we rejoin the present and continue our life in this world with the companionship of others, no longer alone.

Psychodrama

Psychodrama is a type of group counseling that is similar to limbic system therapy. It utilizes small groups and gives us opportunities to have interpersonal experiences we have not had the chance to experience. It is not a form of group therapy where the participants sit in a circle and share their experiences. It is far more dynamic than that. This form of therapy can accomplish far more in one or a few sessions than six months of talk therapy. This is because it opens us up to new experiences that help us rewire our brain. It also can help us work out any unfinished business and get closure with significant others who have been involved in our painful or traumatic experience. Many of the people who have been involved in our painful experiences may no longer be living. Yet, in other instances, they are living but would not be willing participants, either due to not having a mindset healthy enough to help us get closure, or due to a refusal to participate. This type of group therapy gives us the opportunity to go back and re-create the old experiences and relationships so that we can get from others what we should have received in the past.

The setting involves a room, and in some instances a stage. The main participant chooses a scene from their life, often one that was the most painful or troublesome, and then identifies all the people who played a role. Volunteers are selected from the group to play the roles of the people from the past. The therapist is present as the director of the interactions and helps guide the recreating of the story. The main participant, whose story is being acted out, may be sitting or standing, as are the others in the role-play. The therapist may choose to arrange the chairs a certain way as is most helpful. Then the main participant describes the scene and identifies a starting point. This is not a simple reenactment of a past trauma or painful experience. A mere reenacting of what occurred would not be healthy; instead, it is reenacted with a different outcome than what had occurred in the past. In essence, the participants all play a role in the healing of the person whose story is being told and acted out. The therapist helps the main participant identify their thoughts, feelings, and unmet needs from that time and helps them verbalize them to the other participants. Then, gradually, each of the other members responds to the main participant, but in a healing way. They offer messages that should have been said in the past but were not. It can become a very emotional experience. The main participant is often able to obtain the closure they need, move on, unlearn their trauma response, and learn that people can indeed not only be safe, but be healing presences.

Unfortunately, this type of therapy is not available everywhere. It is more of a specialty, and certain geographical areas might not have professionals who are trained in it. However, if these types of therapy groups are not available, there are more widely accessible options, such as smaller role-plays or the empty chair technique, in which we imagine the person we need closure with is present in the empty chair. We can then dialogue with them. We can also take it further by switching roles and imagining *ourselves* in the empty chair while we role-play being the person we need to get closure with, and we give the responses we need to hear. This switching of roles can create a dialogue with someone we would not normally have access to, and it can bring us meaningful closure. It may also help us understand the other person better. The point of these exercises is to give us a deep experience, usually interaction based, that can access all the parts of the brain that were affected by a painful or traumatic experience. Sadly, we do harm one another, but we can also help heal one another. The reality is, we need one another. We cannot heal in isolation. If we have learned to fear others, we can only unlearn that fear by having new experiences that involve others.

Eye Movement Desensitization and Reprocessing (EMDR)

We might find that even after doing so much of this work, we still feel stuck; we still have that nagging feeling that somehow the past is happening all over again in our lives. We might even sense that something from the past is still blocking our perception of the present, and we might still notice that we respond to normal, healthy events in the present as though they are the painful events of the past. We might feel some improvement but that an emotional shadow still looms over us from the past. When this occurs, we may very well feel frustrated; however, there are some real, physiological reasons why we experience this, and EMDR can help.

EMDR was discovered in the early 1980s when Francine Shapiro went for a walk after something had distressed her. As she walked, she noticed that as her eyes moved back and forth from right to left while she thought about what bothered her, she would feel more relaxed and at peace. In time, and after more research to develop what she had discovered, EMDR treatment came into existence. It is very powerful, effective, and faith-friendly. In fact, those who are typically phobic of talk therapy would likely be more comfortable with EMDR. While EMDR involves a therapist, it is not talk therapy—the therapist is primarily there to guide the process.

To understand how EMDR works, we need to remember what was discussed earlier about how traumatic or acutely painful memories are not stored or integrated normally into the brain in such a way that we feel them as memories of the past. Even if we understand on a cognitive level that the memory is of a past event, we feel it emotionally as though it is still occurring. These partially integrated neural networks are also easily triggered by anything in the present that reminds us of or has anything in common with our painful past. What EMDR proposes is that when we say or feel like we cannot let go of the past, there may very well be a real, biological reason. We may *want* to let go of the past, but we might physically be unable to. Perhaps we have a traumatic memory that is stuck, partially integrated, and frozen. It needs something more than self-talk, cognitive therapy, lecturing, or gratitude to become unstuck, integrated, and finally put to rest in the past where it belongs. Through the creation and development of EMDR, it was discovered that rapid back-and-forth eye movement using what is called bilateral stimulation of the eyes helps activate the memory reprocessing process. An analogy we might use is that of a computer and its hard drive. There is a program on computers that allows us to defragment our hard drive so that all the files become organized and get put in their proper places. In essence, this is what EMDR does for our brain. Our brain is the hard drive, and the memories are the files.

An EMDR session begins with us holding a painful image, memory, or belief in our mind. The therapist then holds their two fingers up about twelve inches from our face and begins to move them back and forth as we track the finger movements with our eyes. The bilateral stimulation resumes the memory processing that was disrupted and shut down during the traumatic or painful experience. After a short time, the therapist stops the finger movements and asks us what we see. We then report any images or memories that entered out mind. If we have an image or memory enter our mind before the finger movements stop, we can make a gesture to stop the finger movements and report the image or memory. No interpretation of the image or memory is given. The therapist simply gives a nod or an affirmation and continues the next set of finger movements.

It does not take too long to realize there is a progression taking place. It is as though each image and memory are train stops that allows us to revisit a time and experience from our past. However, since the process keeps moving rapidly, we are not left there too long, and we are awake and fully conscious that we are currently in the present and not the past. Through the images and memories, combined with the bilateral stimulation, we go back in a time machine and revisit the time and place of the painful past. Eventually, as the process continues, the imagery and memories start to become more positive. As the memories are put fully into the past while we are aware of the present, the painful memories suddenly lose that rigidity and inflexibility to new experiences. Eventually, the sets of finger movements bring us to images or thoughts of closure, understanding, and resilience. The painful memories have become reprocessed and fully integrated.

When the process is complete, there is a powerful and profound sense of the past being in the past. In fact, for some it is so powerful that for days we might we feel as though we had just gone back and visited our childhood homes and other places from our past; however, this time with a sense of peace and closure. EMDR can give us the gift of a powerful closure that would not have been possible through talk therapy. So many who use this technique observe that they always *knew* the experience was in the past, but now they *feel* that it is in the past. The successful completion of EMDR leads us to feel more at peace, settled, and grounded in the present. It also deactivates triggers that had been troublesome throughout our lives. This is because we are no longer reacting to neural networks of partially integrated traumatic memories—the memories are now where they belong, with the rest of our memories from the past. As a result, we can engage the present for what it is: the present. This resolves the timeless aspect of the traumatic memories. We no longer feel like a child; we now feel like an adult. A profound clarity and peace emerge.

The changes this experience can create in our lives are profound, and for a time, after the completion of EMDR, we enter a phase of having to get used to a life that is freed from the past. It feels as though something has been exorcised from our life, and it is not unusual to feel mildly down for a few weeks as the closure sets in and we experience a final coming to terms with the life we have been given. During this temporary phase, we may even feel a sense of sadness because we are saying farewell to something that, although painful and distressing, was familiar to us for so long. However, this sadness will pass, and we will become truly freed from the past.

EMDR and Forgiveness

As we let go of the past, we will find that forgiveness is also an important part of the process, but it is difficult. It is especially difficult when memories of our profoundly painful experiences were not integrated properly. How can we know if we have forgiven someone when current experiences feel like painful reoccurrences of past experiences? This inevitably leads to confusion. When memories from a traumatic or painful experience were not integrated properly, we never quite feel safe, and we live in a chronic state of defensive posturing. Therefore, we are too busy defending ourselves and trying to keep ourselves safe, and cannot have the mindset to forgive. Also, forgiveness can be difficult when the past was never put in the past but instead feels timeless, as though it extends into our present life. We might even have done all the emotional, spiritual, and cognitive work needed and have already forgiven, but we doubt that we have, because we are so stuck in the past due to memories that were not integrated fully. Forgiveness is about letting go, but memories that were not integrated properly will not allow us to let go of the past because they dictate our perception of the present. EMDR gives us the gift of letting go. When we can finally see a painful experience as a past event and feel it as a past event, we no longer have to keep that toxic vigil of watching for signs of the past in the present.

In a way, EMDR has a Paschal or resurrectional quality to it. As old painful neural networks become resolved, integrated, and put in the past, our hearts and minds become like the space of the empty tomb: a place where there was once profound sadness and pain becomes a place of peace and understanding. The suffering is no more and is in the past. The former pain that so consumed us has passed away. It is like how we feel after a long Lenten struggle when we finally experience the relief and joy of Bright Week. It is a sense of a new beginning. As our minds and hearts suddenly have more space for the present, due to the receding of our painful past, we develop a greater ability and desire to forgive. This newfound peace radiates outward, and we are no longer afraid to reach out and give humanity a second chance.

CHAPTER 7

Navigating Healing Work

S OME OF US MAY STRUGGLE to envision what healing work
looks like on a day-to-day basis. How frequently should we
do this work? How much time should we spend on it? How can
we know when to keep pushing or when to pause, and be able
to move with the ebbs and flows of healing work? This chapter
addresses these questions.

Moments of distress are often the starting point of our healing work. Such times should be recorded in our journal much
as one might mark a spot on a map. In many ways we are like
an archaeologist seeking the location of a certain artifact. Often
there may be multiple possibilities for where such objects are buried—but an archeologist can only make the discovery by excavating. Likewise, in our moments of distress and disproportionate reactions, we may need to pursue many possible catalysts to
find resolution and healing. We can learn to view our moments
of struggle and distress as opportunities. If we follow the pain,
we can find the cause, and if we can find the cause, we can find
resolution. Giving specific chronological steps to take would be
difficult and unwise, as each one of us is in a different stage of

our healing work, and therefore there will be some variation for each person. Thus, only the general content that our daily healing work should include will be covered. It will be up to the reader to fit it into their lives as is best and most fruitful for them.

By now, having read the earlier chapters, many of us know the origins of our struggles. We may also have some idea as to how they are affecting our daily life. Assessing our healing work is much like putting together a jigsaw puzzle. We sit at a table, and we have all these pieces spread out over it. We can see all the pieces, but we just do not yet know where they all fit. So it is for us. We can often see all the snapshots of our lives, our struggles, our behaviors, and hurts; however, we don't know how they all connect. Our first step is to tolerate this reality. There is no quick fix for healing work. As with the process of putting together a jigsaw puzzle, we will need to exercise patience. However, even though it takes time for the jigsaw puzzle to come together, we do get relief, bit by bit, as each piece fits into place. This provides motivation for us to continue to push ahead and finish the puzzle.

Healing work is the same. It is a process, and it is one we cannot rush. However, each time we achieve some success, it helps build our trust in the process and motivates us to push on. It also builds our self-confidence. Our healing work occurs in layers. As we resolve one layer, we typically experience significant relief. For example, we may notice there are times when our struggle or distress reaches a peak. This might be due to a trigger, a specific event, or to the arrival of a certain life stage. When we can identify why we were triggered, that in fact it is the past we are responding to, and we are able to identify the true origin of our feelings and struggles, we obtain a good amount of relief. This is a victory in what is to be many battles. Once we have one victory, we gain valuable experience, and we gain greater confidence in our ability to do the same again when the next layer of work appears or when a new struggle surfaces.

Often when we experience a victory in our healing work, we must tolerate the uncertainty of not knowing whether our work is complete or whether further struggles are yet to come. It is okay if we do not know; we can savor one victory at a time. We can relish the peace and relief we achieved through a breakthrough in our work and rest at ease, knowing that when the next layer reveals itself, we will be able to work through it. Ultimately, we must become adept at navigating pain and learn to trust the process. It is also important to assign the proper meaning to our emotional pain. We will need to know that our emotional pain is calling us to action, that it does not have to endure forever, and that we have control over it. Our emotional pain is a distress signal that pulsates deep from within. It is not a threat to us—it is our friend and ally, letting us know that an aspect of our inner world needs attention.

Tolerating Our Painful Emotions

Too often we fear emotional pain. We tend to flee from it through avoidance, whether by self-medicating, keeping busy, distracting ourselves, or simply by not thinking about it. As common as this is, it is perhaps the greatest obstacle to our healing work. It is imperative that we revise the meanings we assign to emotional pain and other feelings of discomfort. They are telling us something, not trying to hurt us. We often fall into a mindset where our negative emotions—whether depression, anxiety, fear, or profound sadness—become the boogeymen who randomly show up and try to seize control of our lives. In reality, these painful feelings function similarly to pain from a cavity. The pain itself does not hurt us; it simply tells us we need to tend to something. So it is with emotional pain—we need to act upon it.

If we learn to respond to our emotional pain properly, we become masters of our inner world. It is not unusual to experience an increase in the intensity of emotional pain when we have become ready to resolve it. It is critical to see these moments through and not abandon the process. In other words, we have to trust our emotional pain and follow where it leads us. It is our guide trying to lead us out. We respond properly by asking ourselves, "What are these feelings trying to tell me?" Then we excavate until we find out why we are struggling. We identify what triggered us, the origin of the trigger, and what we need to do to resolve it. It is like when rescue workers are trying to locate victims of an accident or other tragedy. They must often follow signals of some kind to find the site of the rescue. In essence, we have to become our own rescuers. When we begin to feel emotional discomfort, we respond with mercy and compassion. We need to engage it and not avoid it. We lean into it, not away from it. We rush to the scene to render aid and care. Once we gain the knowledge and the skills, we can learn to manage our inner world quite well.

We need the ability to tolerate emotional discomfort because any time we spend in avoidance is time we don't spend healing. If we find this difficult, we can practice sitting quietly with our feelings and focusing on where we feel them in our bodies. We then do an exposure exercise on ourselves and learn to sit with the feelings. We also revise what meaning we are assigning to the pain. If we assign threatening meaning to our emotional pain, then we will have anxiety over our painful feelings, which makes us suffer more than we need and can also make us susceptible to self-medicating. However, when we normalize our emotional pain and respond with gentleness and compassion, it makes the pain less intense, less overwhelming, and more bearable. Going through this process with all negative emotions lessens their intensity.

There is a great paradox to navigating our emotional world. It is precisely when we lean into our feelings, sit with them, and normalize instead of fear them, that we begin to feel better. Our feelings cannot harm us. It's only when we assign a threatening meaning to them that they can cause damage to us. However, even then, it is we—not our feelings—who inadvertently harm ourselves. For example, anxiety is a normal emotion we all have. However, as many of us know, fearing our anxious feelings compounds them and causes us to suffer more. For many, relief from anxiety lies when we reach the point where we can sit with uncomfortable emotions, normalize them, and tolerate rather than fear them.

How We Relate with Ourselves

How we relate with ourselves is of utmost importance in our daily work. We must not shame or get frustrated with ourselves for struggling because struggle is necessary for healing. It is not a sin to struggle. This point is critical. Would we shame others for struggling? Of course not. We are often encouraged to reflect on and be mindful of how we treat others. We also, quite naturally, pay attention to how others treat us. However, we very often pay little attention to how we treat ourselves; we almost entirely overlook this aspect of our lives. Some of us may even have an aversion to practicing awareness of how we relate with ourselves because perhaps it conjures up fears of being egocentric or self-focused. But being aware of how we relate with ourselves helps us make progress in our healing work.

Relating with ourselves means how we perceive ourselves, how we respond to ourselves with our thoughts, how we dialogue with ourselves when we are alone or have quiet moments, and how we respond to and feel about ourselves when we make perceived mistakes. We tend to see that certain themes arise with how we relate with ourselves. Do we tend to be more peaceful, gentle, and positive, or do we tend to shame ourselves? How we relate with ourselves comes from our disposition of heart or our inner disposition. Every Christian's goal is to make sure our inner disposition is that of Christ's: one that is merciful, patient, kind, gentle, affirming, and loving.

In our healing work we are called to show ourselves daily the same mercy and love that Christ Himself shows us. It is not spiritually self-indulgent to be merciful toward ourselves if we apply and practice mercy appropriately. However, some of us constantly and forever punish ourselves and feel badly about ourselves. Many of us relate with ourselves in a very harsh, demanding, and critical way, always feeling bad about everything we do. This is because we feel bad about who we are. This is not what God wants. We are children of God and are made in His image. We must show ourselves the same mercy that Christ would show us, and affirm ourselves in the same way Christ affirms all others.

If we have been abused, we often learn to relate with ourselves in an abusive way. Long after the abuser has left our lives, we continue the abuse without realizing it by relating with ourselves in a harsh and shaming way, just as the abuser conditioned us. If we don't address this, it will be an obstacle to spiritual growth and healing. It is amazing how much more efficiently someone heals and grows spiritually once they cease having a harsh and merciless disposition toward themselves. For example, if we happen to find ourselves feeling depressed, the worst thing we can do is shame ourselves for it. We will only then feel more depressed. However, if we instead say to ourselves, "I am feeling depressed, and that is okay," we may feel less depressed because we are giving ourselves permission to feel what we feel, and we are responding to ourselves with compassion. We can apply this to anxiety and any other painful emotion.

Our harsh and critical disposition toward ourselves can also block those deep experiences that we need to contradict what our painful or traumatic experiences taught us. And our self-abuse can surround our soul with dark clouds that block out the love of God. When those of us who are too hard on ourselves learn to ease up, it is as though rays of light suddenly start to break through as God's love begins to reach our soul. Our Faith is all about balance. We are firm with ourselves, we hold ourselves accountable; but we are also merciful and kind to ourselves. This is especially true when healing from those painful or traumatic experiences that were never our fault. Having a balanced disposition means we will better be able to show love to others and grow spiritually in a more efficient way.

The Ebbs and Flows of Our Work

We will likely notice ebbs and flows to our healing work, and this is normal. Our mind, and God Himself, knows the pace at which we need to move. We may make great progress and ascents, only then to reach a leveling out. Often breakthroughs are followed by plateaus, or pauses, as we assimilate the recent healing and resolution into our lives. During these pauses, we may find ourselves wondering if we are done or if there will be more work to do. Sometimes it feels like we are finished and healed, but then our struggles surface again months, or even a year, later. It may feel like the same struggle but with slight variations. Then again, it might be a different struggle than what we experienced before. This happens because sometimes we might think we have resolved a core struggle when in fact we have only peeled back one layer. We find ourselves pausing and assimilating our progress; however, later the next layer will reveal itself, and we will realize our work is not over. What determines the pauses in between is a mystery. It is different for each one of us.

This kind of gradual, layered healing may not occur for all of us, though. If our painful or traumatic experiences were not chronic, or there was a singular, more acute experience, we may not experience healing in this way. In such instances, we might find that we get right to the core experience and obtain resolution in a shorter period of time. But if we experienced chronic dysfunction in our childhood that went on for years, it may take longer to identify all the ways it has affected our present life, what meanings we have assigned to it, what fears we have developed, what we are avoiding, and what our triggers are. In other words, we just have more ground to cover. However, by knowing what to look for, and with the right focus and treatment, we can reduce the time it takes to heal from an experience.

We would also do well to not underestimate the impact of busyness and distraction on our healing work. Inevitably, we will all experience periods of time when we must put our healing work on pause. Sometimes it may be for days, and other times it could last for months. Perhaps it is just a busy season at work, or there are too many things going on at once during a certain time of year. We need to keep in mind, however, that being busy can sometimes mask our struggles or the pain we are feeling. Deliberately keeping busy can be a form of avoidance and self-medicating. Even when we become too busy just by circumstance, not due to avoidance, we can be lured into a sense that we are better and do not need to do any further work. This is because, even when our distraction is involuntary, it still consumes our focus, attention, and thus our emotions. However, it is only a matter of time before this catches up to us. Inevitably, after some weeks or months, our emotional pain will begin to come out sideways and we will feel anxious, down, overwhelmed, or out of control, or we will experience somatic symptoms. So, it is important that even when we enter a busy time, we deliberately check in on our work, whether by reviewing what we have accomplished so far or by continuing to plug away at resolution. We need balance. It is okay to keep busy and productive if our behavior is not avoidance, but in the end, we do need to take breaks so that we can attend to our healing work.

Reading the Mirror of Resonance

We have all had moments where something has resonated with us, or moved us in a very deep way. However, the moments of resonance that occur when we need healing tend to be more powerful and stronger in intensity. We could be perfectly fine one moment, and then suddenly we are overcome with emotion because something we encountered just grabbed us and squeezed our heart. These moments of resonance tend to trigger feelings of hurt and pain, and often result in tears, but they can be great blessings and provide opportunities for us. When we engage and learn from them, they can help us leap ahead in our healing work. These moments are clues. They mirror back an aspect of ourselves that we need to access but haven't yet, because we did not know they were there. A moment of resonance can give us in minutes what normally would have taken a year to accomplish or discover.

When something resonates with us, it means it has gotten past defenses we have employed to keep certain experiences or emotions at bay. A resonating moment has a mysterious way of disabling our defenses. We can spend a lifetime avoiding certain memories, emotions, or experiences, only to have them accessed and the corresponding emotion brought up because we have seen or heard some aspect of our pain in something or someone else. We could be watching a movie and see a scene where someone experiences grief and suddenly, we cry in a very profound way. Or we might see a scene where a desperate person is seeking help from another person, or from God in prayer, and we find ourselves mysteriously getting emotional. We might witness a scene in a movie where the character, despite experiencing many setbacks, pushes forward with courage, perseveres, and emerges victorious, and we can't get enough of watching it. We may even feel unusually drawn to such movies or books, deem them our favorites, and never grow tired of watching or reading them. When these moments of resonance occur, we are often stunned by their effect, and we respond by asking ourselves why we feel this way. Or we might be quick to dismiss these moments as silly and let them pass by without further inspection. But that would be a tragedy and a lost opportunity because they offer us a glimpse into core unresolved pockets of emotion and, as mentioned above, give us a shortcut to a core aspect of our experience that we haven't processed. Calling to mind the analogy of the archaeologist from earlier in this chapter, moments of resonance are like dynamite that can blast through layers and allow us to find that which we seek.

However, to capitalize on these moments, we must engage them and not avoid them. We do this by asking ourselves what the specific theme was of the experience we observed or heard that so resonated. These moments can convey what we cannot or have not yet been able to verbalize. For example, perhaps we have simply been feeling overwhelmed but have not acknowledged it, and we then witness someone on television expressing emotions related to feeling overwhelmed. Or perhaps the resonance reflects something not as simple and much deeper. For example, we might have suffered a loss early in our life that is unresolved, then we watch a movie that depicts someone finally grieving or coming to terms with a loss, and that is a grief trigger for us. (And remember, loss comes in all shapes, forms, and sizes.) In essence, the character in the movie is feeling what we need to feel, but we have not allowed ourselves to do so. During these moments, a window opens that gives us a glimpse into our true, and often most core, struggles, and we can use this as a guide. Whatever the character's experience and our corresponding emotional response tell us about ourselves can then become our new area of focus—or even our new starting point.

Resonance also operates in group settings. This is called limbic resonance. There is a therapeutic benefit to hearing others share experiences we can relate to, whether we relate to their whole story or just one aspect of it. When we hear someone else's experience that has common elements with our own, and we witness their emotions, it can activate our own limbic system. This is healthy. We were created this way. We need one another. Here is one common example of limbic resonance in action: we might be stressed or feeling overwhelmed by a situation. When we encounter someone who is struggling with a similar experience and feeling just as we do, it is not a mere cognitive validation that takes place. It also feels emotionally comforting and soothing, and it helps to regulate and balance us. We feel better and less overwhelmed when we know we are not the only ones who feel a certain way. We do not look to others to discover how we should feel, but just knowing someone else feels what we do decreases our isolation and creates a sense that others share our experience. It helps us know that we are not alone.

We tend to follow resonance in our lives. We are drawn to it on a deep, unconscious level. Even if we have not been actively trying to address past pain or resolve the unresolved in our lives, there is a significant chance that on an unconscious level, we are seeking resolution and healing in some form by looking for that which resonates with us. This resonance could be evident in a vocation we choose, or a hobby, the types of movies and books we pick, or even our relationship choices. This does not mean that the activities, topics, or people we are drawn to are misplaced or false, or that we are misguided in any way; it simply means there is a reason why they have so much extra meaning to us. In other words, whether we will it or not, our minds will seek and push for resolution of all that is unresolved.

What is unresolved deep within us naturally seeks release, much like a splinter. Even though it is an inanimate object, it naturally works its way out. Our defenses attempt to hold the unresolved in, but we are beings created with a natural inclination to heal. This is part of the image of God in us. This does not only apply to severely painful or traumatic events in our lives but really to any profoundly negative, significant life experience that we have been subjected to. Learning to become aware of that which resonates, and why it resonates, can save us great amounts of time and bring us swifter relief.

When the Past Covers the Present

Often our emotional pain is most acute when we experience feelings from a different time and place. When we learn to explore the answer to the question, "When is the first time I felt those feelings?" more often than not, we will see that we first felt them when we were younger. As mentioned earlier, we can feel very overwhelmed and confused when we re-experience unresolved childhood emotions in our adult life. When negative emotion comes from the present, such as in response to a current stressor, it has a straightforward nature to it, and we tend to not feel confused. Our emotions are proportionate, and we clearly know the stressor. However, unresolved emotions from the past tend to feel overwhelming and disproportionate because our emotions and the stressor do not match up. Engaging in the act of separating the past and present, and learning to discern between the two, is a common activity during for healing work. Often, the moment we become aware that our overwhelming feelings come from the past, we feel an immense amount of relief. This is because we now understand why we feel the disproportionate feelings, and we can see the past and present each for what they are individually. This helps us feel more in control and not overwhelmed. It is like trying to resolve a problem with some electronic equipment, but all the cables are tangled together. We cannot figure out where each cable comes from. However, once we have all the cables untangled, and we can see where each belongs, we can set about resolving the problem.

Rooting Out Control and Avoidance

As we make our way on the healing path, we will need to keep a constant eye out for forms of unhealthy control and avoidance. The two, though seemingly separate and different, actually go hand in hand. Excessive need for control is the avoidance of lack of control, so control can be considered a form of avoidance. Avoidance comes with a heavy cost because it can rob us of the very experiences that heal us, and it can keep us trapped in the past. When we chronically struggle with avoidance, we live according to an old song of the past rather than the present. When we have been deeply hurt, we can fall into avoidance patterns where we stay away from anyone and anything that reminds us of our past unresolved experience. This usually means we avoid a good deal of humanity and many life experiences. The more we avoid, the more our avoidance reinforces the negative beliefs we developed because of our painful experiences. When we sidestep what we fear, we refuse to give humanity another chance. We punish those in the present, and ourselves, for the actions of those in the past. There is an adage in the counseling field: "Do the thing you fear, and the death of that fear will be certain." To put the past in the past, we will need to immerse ourselves in that which we have come to fear. We need to give the present the chance to give us new healing experiences that can bring our brain and nervous system back in line with it.

Control also keeps us from healing in the present. While control is almost universally appealing, it is a burden and comes with a heavy cost that is not sustainable long-term. When we have suffered from painful experiences where we had no control, we can develop an intense need and craving for control in some or all areas of our lives. This need can manifest itself in a need to control others, events, or our own emotions. There might be times when it seems we do have control. However, it is only a matter of time before we cannot maintain that control, and we feel victimized all over again, as though the past is replaying itself. Also, there is a great paradox when it comes to control. We convince ourselves that if we can just maintain absolute control in our lives, we will be at peace and feel safe. In fact, the opposite is true. We are actually at greater risk of re-victimizing ourselves when we pursue control because it is a lost cause. It is mission impossible. This means that the more we try and control, the worse we will feel. It is exhausting, stressful and burdensome, and it is just too much work. And the need for control can become so consuming that it causes us to focus on things that will never heal us. Instead of allowing ourselves to do the work we need to do to find healing, we are perpetually on guard and watching for danger, and we live according to a past unresolved experience.

Thus, we cannot underestimate the importance of embracing *not* being in control because when we try to control what we cannot, we are not actually in control. We are out of control. The only way to gain control is to let go of our need for it. When we let go and embrace our lack of control, we let go of the past and we give our present life a chance. The reverberations of this in our mind, heart, soul, and limbic system are powerful and healing. So, when we become aware of situations in which we are trying to maintain unhealthy control, we must do the opposite. If we fear not being in control, then we must deliberately practice not being in control. It is the only way out of the shadows of the past. Every time we over-function, every time we become controlling, we set ourselves back in our healing and reinforce a past experience, almost becoming slaves to it. While it is indeed a leap of faith, it can be very liberating to give ourselves permission to stand down and not be the great manager of others and the world. Healing takes place in the form of learning to trust humanity—and the ebb and flow of life—once again.

Finding the Experiences That Heal the Brain: Giving Humanity a Second Chance

To fully heal, we will also need to find the deep experiences that can access and heal the same parts of our brain that were affected by traumatic or painful experiences. Oftentimes, these deep experiences already exist in our life, but we overlook them or take them for granted. Perhaps we are employed in a healthy workplace, but we have never allowed ourselves to feel safe in that environment. Or we may have people in our lives who are more than willing to love and affirm us, and would even protect us if we needed them to; however, we have not allowed them to do so because we keep them at a distance. We do not see them for who they are but for who we fear they could become: someone who will hurt us as we have been hurt in the past. We fear that if we allow others to get close, we will just end up being hurt all over again. So often, we even react this way to our own families. When we are listening to the past, living in accordance with it, or trying to prove a belief wrong that we learned in the past, we can often overlook healing experiences in the present, even those in our own homes. We might have been unknowingly rejecting our family's healing messages and affirmations. This is tragic because to heal we need to allow ourselves to be loved and to feel safe.

When someone attempts to love or affirm us, we might also react as though this experience is not real or safe because on a deep, unconscious level we believe that at our core we are unlovable. In this case, we can experience a profound incongruence when others try to love, affirm, or look out for us. It is as though they are giving us a gift, but we cannot accept it because we believe we are unworthy. This tends to indicate the presence of shame. We need to remember that everyone is lovable, including ourselves. So, we learn to give humanity a second chance: both ourselves and others.

This is the great paradox for those of us on the healing path. The very humanity that so failed us or hurt us is the same humanity we need to heal us. We cannot detour around or escape this reality. Of course, God could heal us directly; however, He created us to be interconnected with one another. He does not want us to live alone and isolated. To remain distant and guarded from humanity means we will never truly love and fulfill the great commandment. We have no choice but to love and be loved freely and in a carefree spirit. This is a key part to overriding the fear area of our brain so that we have a chance to have those healing experiences. At our best, we can become fellow physicians of our souls for each other. Certainly, there is always a chance, and a likely one, that we will experience disappointment and be hurt again. However, we come to know that even though we feel similar emotions to those of the past, it is not the same experience happening again.

We also come to learn that we can be hurt again, but still safe. Considering this, we might even welcome disappointing experiences. They allow us to be tested and to realize that although hurt and disappointment occur in the present, that does not mean the past is repeating itself. We are not the vulnerable child or the powerless victim anymore. There have been changes—our life has changed, *we* have changed. We have gained wisdom and experience—time has moved on, and so must we as well. We have resources we did not have before. We can make adult choices, we can set boundaries, we have more emotional literacy, we can troubleshoot ourselves, and we can become our own managers of our emotional world. As we gain confidence in these truths, we become even more resilient. We begin to live like someone who never had the painful experiences that we had. The painful music from the past has ceased. We hear and listen only to the beautiful music of the present where there are risks, but the benefits far outweigh the risks. When this occurs, we have found healing.

Afterword

THE CONSEQUENCES OF ENDEAVORING TO complete the work discussed here go far beyond ourselves. We would do well to remember that each person in our world also has a life story, and our stories have the ability to encounter and affect one another. We also have the power to add to or disrupt another person's life story, depending on the decisions we make. We may think we would have to do something quite dramatic in the life of another to make ourselves significant enough to be part of their story. However, we quite often have the opportunity to affect the trajectory of someone else's life story in smaller ways, and the more we progress in our own healing work, the more we can focus on responding well to every soul we encounter.

If we have reached a point of complete resolution in our lives, we will find that because of our experience and struggle, we have a greater awareness of others. We have grown in the ability to give each soul we meet something different than the world gives. Encountering people who have weathered suffering and pain, and have arrived at a place of peace, tends to be healing even in very small ways. We can even say that healing is contagious. When a wounded soul encounters another soul that has trodden the healing path, resonance occurs. The one who was once wounded but now healed communicates nonverbal messages that they are safe and can soothe. There is a peace that surrounds those who are healed that draws in those who need peace. Indeed, our own healing work can act as a lighthouse in the dark to those who hurt, offering hope that peace can be found.

We can also offer healing to our families. Every family needs a healer. It may be many generations before one appears in a family, but it is beautiful when it happens. In many ways we could say that there is something heroic about the one who takes up that cause. The family healer is usually one who possesses a variety of traits that causes them to take on that role, such as sensitivity, emotional intelligence, love, gentleness, depth of heart, and courage. The healer also possesses a profound sense of right and wrong, and a good sense of what is healthy and what is not.

We all have the ability not only to pursue our own healing but the healing of those before us and even those not yet born. Until a healer arises in a family where trauma and dysfunction have been passed down, hurt and pain will continue to be transmitted to future generations. When we take up the mantle of family healer, we can break the cycle, stop the dysfunction, and allow new family members to be born and raised who have life stories that are free from the family's inherited pain. When we shoulder pain and push forward, our efforts are not only for our relief, but for all of humanity. Considering this, we can see that our own willingness to face pain and wade through that emotional space between anger and happiness is quite heroic.

Any of us has the ability to become this kind of hero, even though we may encounter many difficulties borne out of our past experiences. We can feel set apart from the rest of humanity when we have suffered profoundly painful experiences. We may have a distorted perception of others who we assume did not suffer painful experiences, and we can sometimes struggle to make sense of this. Sadly, many assign the meaning to this perception that we simply were not good enough for a normal life. We feel set apart as though we were never worthy of that. This can leave us with the burden of feeling not good enough and as though we are defective. However, we must reframe the meanings assigned to these perceptions. It is not that we were not worthy or good enough. Indeed, through our experiences, we have received a calling for something higher and quite admirable because not only do we have the *ability* to be a hero, we have been called to that. We can be a hero who has emerged from our experience with a noble emotional bearing, a quiet strength, wisdom, deep peace, and a profound resilience. These traits also offer us our proverbial victory wreath for our healing work that we fought hard for with dignity. Once we have experienced the dignity that comes with a heroic healing, we display a stubborn refusal to ever again feel as we once did. This is not pride. It is actually rooted in humility. We simply have worked too hard to go back to feeling as we once did. We also tend to have a powerful conscience that, out of a sense of duty to those around us, will not let us go back. Our time on the healing path has given us a heavy dose of reality and forced us to see ourselves as we really are. We see that dignity is a fruit of humility, not of pride. Truly, there are no treasures on earth worth such qualities.

Of course, this heroism is not all or nothing. Perhaps we tried our best and managed to allow family pain to reach our children only in small forms. In such instances, while we might have made small mistakes, overall, we stopped the bulk of the family's pain and dysfunction from getting through to the next generation. We were willing to confront and work through painful emotions beyond happiness and anger, so that they might have peace. And we need to remember that while a hero is someone who rescues others from danger, we do not need to wait for a situation of crisis or danger to arise to prove our willingness to be a hero. The opportunity for heroism exists now. The healing path is the path to heroism. When we take up the calling to heal ourselves, we protect the next generations from the danger of bearing pain for deeds they were not responsible for, even though we ourselves had to bear that pain. Each of us has the invitation to become the family healer. Indeed, the calling to heroism is a universal calling.

APPENDIX A

Example of a Life Story Written in Timeline Format

My life began in 1978 in a small, rural town in Pennsylvania.

My father worked and I rarely saw him. My mother had a drinking problem.

I know it is associated with my home environment growing up.

I feel I am still looking for someone to take care of me instead of always being the caretaker.

I keep waiting for someone to take care of me.

I know my mother loved me, but I always felt like I was losing her.

I have periods of time where I seem to feel sad and I don't know why.

I've been a good mother and wife, and I've made sure my children have never had to experience what I did.

In taking care of others, I have neglected myself. I've done this my whole life.

I realize I have conditioned my family to perceive that I don't need anything and that I am independent.
I need to assert my needs more.

I need to grieve the loss of what I should have had when I was a child.

APPENDIX B

Example of a Life Narrative Written in Paragraph Format

I WAS BORN IN 1956 in a town in northern Ohio to Ron and Louisa. I had two older siblings, a brother and a sister.

For as long as I can remember, my parents fought sporadically, but when they did fight, the arguments were severe and frightening. I would often hide during the fights while my two siblings tried to separate my parents and stop the fighting. While hiding, I would hear terrible sounds and screams. It would sound as though my mother were being killed. I could hear my siblings yelling "No, no!" Then there would be silence. Eventually, my siblings would come down to check on me, and I would always ask if my mom was going to be okay. They would reassure me and guide me back to my room. My father would leave the house. My mother would be emotionally incapacitated from these fights, and my siblings would help her to bed. I remember just wanting to make sure my mom was okay. My father did not kill my mother, but I would hear him, in the heat of a terrible argument, say that he would kill her. Those threats, combined with the sounds and not being able to see what was happening, made me feel like my mom was being killed even though that never actually occurred. I recall that the rest of the night the atmosphere in the house would be full of grief—a palpable, unspoken sense that something had happened that should not have. There was a profound sense of tragedy.

The next day we would be expected to go to school like nothing had happened. Strangely enough, my parents could never understand why my grades were not good. They subjected me to an abnormal environment but expected normalcy from me. There would be times, even weeks, of calm and quiet, but this would eventually end with a terrible evening of fighting. Then some more weeks of calm.

As I grew older, my siblings went off to college, and I lived alone with my parents. When my parents would fight, I had to intervene. I remember feeling powerless. I couldn't get them to stop fighting. Around this time, during my teenaged years, my father became emotionally and verbally abusive toward me. He spent many hours on weekends shut in his bedroom while he gambled on football games. At times, if he lost, he would come downstairs in a foul mood and take it out on us. He couldn't tolerate seeing my mother be affectionate with me and would often yell at my mother to "stop babying him." I didn't understand it then, but I see now that my father had not had a good relationship with his own mother—her behavior toward him was emotionally abusive. When my father would see my mother being affectionate with me, it would remind him of what he didn't have, and it would set him off. I see clearly now that my father was a wounded soul who never did any healing work. I do recall, right around age fifteen and when my father's emotional abuse toward me peaked, my self-esteem and self-confidence plummeted. However, I recall when I was sixteen, I started defending myself against my father.

In my later adolescence, when I was eighteen and a senior in high school, my parents separated. Both of my siblings had already left the house. The divorce was finalized several years later. Whenever I would see one parent, they would complain about the other. I was often asked to relay messages between them. My father was a narcissist and passive aggressive. If there was anything he could do to prevent and disrupt my mother from having a normal life, he would do so. The post-separation years were sad ones, and a deep sense of brokenness and loss hung over my family. We were all scattered, and we would never have that sense of wholeness again that intact families have.

Eventually I went off to school, and my mother lived alone. I often worried about her. Every so many weeks my father would call and rage about something that my mother was doing. He could never seem to let me have a normal life. I do recall, during some of these conversations, that I would plead for normalcy and ask why we couldn't just have a normal father-son relationship. He could not answer, and there would be a heavy silence on the phone. In hindsight, it is clear to me now the answer was that he had never had a normal relationship with his father, but he did not have the self-awareness to verbalize this. Over time, I noticed my father becoming calmer and milder as he aged, beginning in his late fifties. He eventually lost his business and worked an assortment of odd jobs. After a while, he could not afford to live alone and had to move in with his mother, which was the ultimate humiliation for him. He had hit rock bottom.

Eventually I moved home with my mother, and up until this point, there seemed to be no signs that I had suffered any significant wounds from these experiences. After some years, I got married and started a family. As the early years of having a family passed, and I was in my mid-thirties, I began to sense there were wounds that needed to be healed. It was just a vague sense that something was off and needed to be repaired. I was overly sensitive and struggled if my wife was in a negative mood. Others told me I didn't allow people to be cranky without personalizing it—they seemed to feel that I expected people to always be in a good mood and wouldn't allowed them to have an "off" day. It didn't take long for me to know where this had come from. I was a great father and spent much time with my kids. I played with them, but always felt a profound sense of loss and sadness when I did. The sense of loss perplexed me, as I did not experience any unusual deaths in my life. I also felt a bit hypervigilant, always on the lookout for something to go wrong and struggling to be in the present moment instead of fixating on potential negative events on the horizon.

Once, there was a tragic school shooting in the news. The children were very young. I had a profound grief reaction to this event. Most people were upset by it, but it seemed more intense for me, like there was something extra in my grief. What I was feeling seemed heavier and sadder, almost like I had experienced the shooting firsthand or the children who had died were my own. I soon realized what grieved me the most was the loss of normalcy and safety that the children had experienced and the unshakable sense that they had gone through something that just shouldn't have happened in the first place. I quickly realized the event was tapping into some unresolved grief from my childhood, my own loss of normalcy, and the things I myself had experienced that should not have happened.

This began a period of one-and-a-half to two years of grieving and processing everything that had happened during my childhood. I had never grieved it and so had to go back and do so now. About six months later, after much grief work, I noticed that I felt lighter and more cheerful. I also understood why I sometimes felt sad when I played with my kids. Raising them activated my own unresolved pain from my childhood—I was giving my kids a life I had not received myself. Soon, that sadness I felt when playing with my kids went away.

After much counseling and applying cognitive behavioral therapy, I learned specifically how I was affected by my early experiences. I learned how they affected my beliefs about myself, others, God, and the world. I also realized I had engaged in self-blame as a child and carried the egocentric belief into adulthood that bad things happen because of me. As a result of addressing this, I no longer felt guilty when negative things happened in my adulthood that I had no control over. I became aware that I was carrying a massive amount of shame due to the self-blame that I engaged in. Soon, the shame lifted, and I felt much lighter. I was able to practice better self-compassion and relate with myself in healthier ways. I also noticed my hypervigilance began to weaken and fade. I was more relaxed and able to be in the present moment.

However, I kept being intentional about healing work for the next eight years, and I continue to do so. I learned to recognize my triggers—events or experiences that can make me feel like I did in the past. However, these have improved as I continue to learn more about myself and gain insight and self-awareness. I have begun changing how I respond to these triggers, which is creating new experiences for me and helping me learn new ways to relate. I also learned that I have some traits of a parentified child. I learned these traits or this role by assuming responsibility for situations growing up that I had no control over. I learned to try and control the uncontrollable. This is what parentified children do. The three roles I learned were to: 1) Protect my mother and make sure she was okay; 2) Stop conflict and fights by making sure no one got upset, which led to people pleasing; 3) Believe that it was my job to protect my family and hold my family together. It is clear to me now how I learned these three roles from my childhood home environment. I realized that whenever I could not do one of these roles, I felt shame, and my self-confidence would plummet. Later in my life I had to come to terms with the reality that I cannot fulfill those roles; it is impossible. Also, I learned that I should never have been in those roles. I had to learn to let them go. There was grief in coming to terms with this, and it is a process.

APPENDIX C

Exercise 1: Assigning Percentages to Current Stressors

The objective of Exercise 1 is to create a pie graph of our present stress. The participant needs to identify the sources of their present stress and assign each source a portion of the pie equal to the proportion it is taking. This simple exercise can give us relief because we see our stress, which has felt so overwhelming and abstract, suddenly organized and contained on a piece of paper. It can help us feel less overwhelmed and enable us to strategize how to begin resolving what we can.

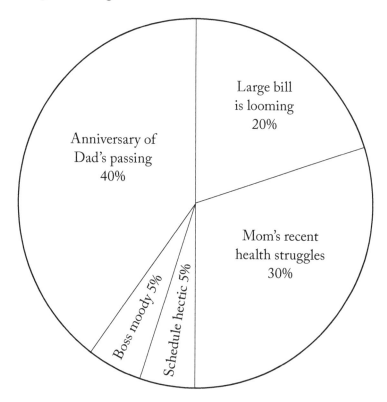

Large bill
is looming
20%

Anniversary of
Dad's passing
40%

Mom's recent
health struggles
30%

Boss moody 5%

Schedule hectic 5%

Figure 1: How Insight Leads to Resolution

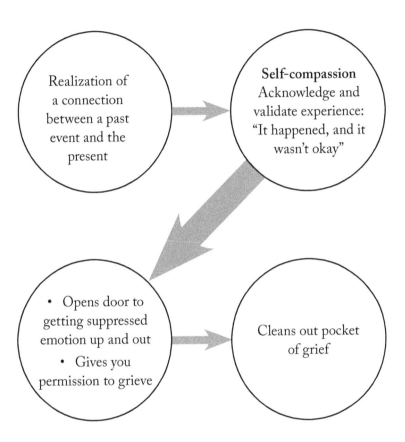

Exercise 2: Connecting Events and Emotions

Exercise 2 can help us begin practicing insight. It requires us to sit with ourselves, pause, look within, and start sorting out what we are feeling and why. To complete Exercise 2, create two columns on a piece of paper. In the first column, list events or stressors that are affecting your thoughts and emotions. In the second column, list the negative emotions you have been struggling with. Then, draw lines connecting the event or stressor with the emotion it is responsible for. This allows us to see which emotion seems most prevalent, as certain emotions will have more lines drawn to them. It also helps us validate what we have been struggling with in our lives. It is important to note that in this table, we can see there are normal reactions to everyday stressful events. However, it also contains emotional responses to events that can be evidence of an unresolved past.

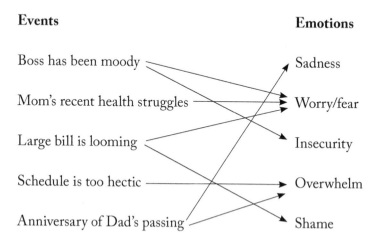

APPENDIX D

Examples of Core Beliefs

Core Beliefs Related to Helplessness

I am weak.	I am a failure.
I am not good enough.	I am defective.
I am incompetent.	I am inadequate.
I am powerless.	I am at the mercy of others.
I am vulnerable.	I can affect nothing.

Core Beliefs Related to Unlovability

I am unworthy.

I am not good enough.	I am unlovable.
I am unwanted.	I have nothing to offer.
I am undesirable.	I am bad.
I will be rejected.	I am different.

Core Beliefs About the World (Our General Environment)

The world is not safe.	The world is out of control.
The world is overwhelming.	The world will reject me.
The world will hurt me.	The world is all bad.
The world is overpowering.	The world will punish me.
The world is hostile.	The world will take from me.

Core Beliefs About Others

Others will hurt me.	Others will betray me.
Other people are not safe.	Others will turn on me.
Others will lose interest in me.	Others cannot be trusted.
Others will reject me.	Others do not love me.
Others are better than me.	Others will disappoint me.

Examples of Conditional Beliefs/Attitudes

» If I do not get close to others, I can keep myself safe.

» As long as I do not get close to others, I can never be rejected.

» So long as I work hard and please others, no one will ever get upset.

» As long as I can always prove I am good enough, I will have self-worth.

» If I can keep others at a distance, they will never see my defects and flaws.

» As long as I do not get close to people, I will not disappoint them.

» If I can control the uncontrollable, then nothing bad will ever happen.

» If I can control the uncontrollable, then I will never feel powerless and weak again.

» If I can control the uncontrollable, then I will have self-worth.

» If I can keep others happy, then there will never be conflict.

» If I punish myself through depriving myself of joy and

affirmation, then God will not have to punish me.

» If I can maintain absolute control over all areas of my life, then I will be safe.

» If I can please others, then they will want me around.

Examples of Automatic Thoughts

I hate myself.	I should just leave.
I am ugly.	No one loves me.
Why would someone want to be around me?	
God doesn't love me.	
I am bad.	I'm strange.
I can't do anything right.	I have nothing to offer.
I am so annoying.	They will not like me.
No one wants to be around me.	Things never work out.
I can't trust anyone.	I'm no good.
What if I get hurt?	I have no one.
What if I'm not in control?	I can't trust anyone.
What if they don't include me?	Life is so not fair.
Nothing ever works out.	I am always being punished.

Exercise 3: Downward Arrow Exercise

At a meeting at work, I overheard my manager praise a coworker. I was fine until that point, then afterward my mood dramatically deteriorated.

↓

It upset me because it meant my manager was pleased with my coworker and not me.

↓

And if my manager was pleased with my coworker and not me, that means my manager was disappointed in me.

↓

And if my manager was disappointed in me, that means I did something wrong.

↓

And if I did something wrong, that means I wasn't good enough.

↓

And if I wasn't good enough, that means I failed.

Bibliography

Beck, Judith S. *Cognitive Behavior Therapy, Third Edition: Basics and Beyond.* New York: The Guilford Press, 2020.

Buczynski, Ruth. *Treating Trauma Master Series.* With Bessel van der Kolk, Pat Ogden, Ruth Lanius, Dan Siegel, Stephen Porges, Allen Schore, and Peter Levine. Online Training Module. National Institute for the Clinical Application of Behavioral Medicine. https://www.nicabm.com/confirm/ treating-trauma-master-2/.

Levine, Peter A., and Maggie Kline. *Trauma Through a Child's Eyes: Awakening the Ordinary Miracle of Healing—Infancy through Adolescence.* Berkeley, CA: North Atlantic Books, 2007.

Levine, Peter A. *Trauma and Memory: Brain and Body in a Search for the Living Past: A Practical Guide for Understanding and Working with Traumatic Memory.* Berkeley, CA: North Atlantic Books, 2015.

Nellas, Panayiotis. *Deification in Christ: Orthodox Perspectives on the Nature of the Human Person.* Translated by Norman Russell. Crestwood, NY: St. Vladimir's Seminary Press, 1987.

Ogden, Pat, Kekuni Minton, and Clare Pain. *Trauma and the Body: A Sensorimotor Approach to Psychotherapy.* New York: W. W. Norton & Company, 2006.

Salas, Jesus A. *Getting Better Every Day: The Client's Guide to Cognitive Behavioral Therapy Treatment.* Meadville, PA: Fulton Books, 2020.

Schmemann, Alexander. *For the Life of the World.* Crestwood, NY: St. Vladimir's Seminary Press, 2018.

Schmemann, Alexander. *Of Water & the Spirit: A Liturgical Study of Baptism.* Crestwood, NY: St. Vladimir's Seminary Press, 1997.

Shapiro, Francine, and Margot Silk Forest. *EMDR: The Breakthrough Therapy for Overcoming Anxiety, Stress, and Trauma.* New York: Basic Books, 2016.

Shapiro, Francine. *Eye Movement Desensitization and Reprocessing (EMDR) Therapy, Third Edition: Basic Principles, Protocols, and Procedures.* New York: The Guilford Press, 2017.

van der Kolk, Bessel A., Alexander C. McFarlane, and Lars Weisaeth, eds. *Traumatic Stress: The Effects of Overwhelming Experience on Mind, Body, and Society.* New York: The Guilford Press, 2006.

Wolynn, Mark. *It Didn't Start with You: How Inherited Family Trauma Shapes Who We Are and How to End the Cycle.* New York: Penguin Books, 2017.

We hope you have enjoyed and benefited from this book. Your financial support makes it possible to continue our nonprofit ministry both in print and online. Because the proceeds from our book sales only partially cover the costs of operating **Ancient Faith Publishing** and **Ancient Faith Radio**, we greatly appreciate the generosity of our readers and listeners. Donations are tax deductible and can be made at **www.ancientfaith.com.**

To view our other publications,
please visit our website: **store.ancientfaith.com**

 ANCIENT FAITH RADIO

Bringing you Orthodox Christian music, readings, prayers, teaching, and podcasts 24 hours a day since 2004 at
www.ancientfaith.com